WRITE YOUR WAY INTO COLLEGE

MASTER THE
SAT ESSAY

OTHER TITLES OF INTEREST FROM LEARNINGEXPRESS

Write Your Way into College: College Admissions Essay
Writing Skills Success in 20 Minutes a Day, 4th Edition
Write Better Essays in 20 Minutes a Day, 2nd Edition
Grammar Success in 20 Minutes a Day, 2nd Edition

WRITE YOUR WAY INTO COLLEGE
MASTER THE SAT ESSAY

LEARNINGEXPRESS®

NEW YORK

Library of Congress Cataloging-in-Publication Data
Write your way into college : master the SAT essay.
        p. cm.
  Includes bibliographical references.
  ISBN 978-1-57685-734-2
 1. English language—Composition and exercises—Examinations—Study guides.
2. SAT (Educational test)—Study guides. I. LearningExpress (Organization)
  LB2353.57.W75 2010
  378.1'662—dc22

                                        2010022246

Printed in the United States of America

9 8 7 6 5 4 3 2 1

First Edition

ISBN 10: 1-57685-734-4
ISBN 13: 978-1-57685-734-2

For information or to place an order, contact LearningExpress at:
  2 Rector Street
  26th Floor
  New York, NY 10006

Or visit us at:
  www.learnatest.com

Direct any questions or comments to:
customerservice@learningexpressllc.com

Contents

CONTENTS

CONTENTS

Contributor ▶

Lauren Starkey is an author, editor, and educator. She has written 20 books, including *How to Write Great Essays*, *SAT Writing Essentials*, *Goof Proof College Admissions Essays*, and test prep titles for the SAT, GRE, LSAT, and MCAT. Lauren created and leads SAT Bootcamp—4 Hours to a Higher Score (www. satbootcamp.us), a New England-based test strategy workshop that's now in its fourth year. She also writes a column on college admissions for www.examiner. com, and provides customized test prep and college essay counseling for individual students. Lauren lives in Vermont with her husband and three children.

Introduction ▶

The *Write your Way into College* series by LearningExpress is about two essays—the SAT essay and the college admissions essay. One is timed, one you can take months to write. One is anonymous, and the other is personal. One scores high when it adheres to specific principles, one gets points for originality. Knowing which is which and how specifically to tackle each essay are the focuses of this book and its companion, *Write Your Way into College: College Admissions Essay.*

Many students panic when they think about writing a complete essay in 25 minutes. In fact, the SAT essay seems to cause more alarm than any other section of the test. But here's the good news: The readers who score your essay aren't expecting incredible writing. They know that under the time constraint you won't be able to spend much time thinking in-depth about your subject or revising what you write. Instead, they're looking for a polished rough draft, one that addresses the essay prompt in an organized way, takes a side on the issue presented and backs it up with examples, evidence, and details.

You'll notice that this book contains a number of practice exercises and writing sessions. The exercises are designed to help you practice and retain what you've learned, as well as to fine-tune the essay content you develop along the way. Writing sessions replicate the space you'll be given to write the SAT essay.

The most important information you'll learn from this book, however, is the importance of making a plan for your essay and following it, no matter what the prompt. It's that well-rehearsed plan that will help you relax and get down to the business of writing a higher scoring essay.

In Chapter 1, we'll explain the polished rough draft in greater detail and answer many of your other SAT essay questions. You'll learn how the essay is scored, what kind of essay you'll be asked to write, how to budget your time, and more. Chapter 2 takes you step-by-step through content development. Choosing topics and researching them before your test date will help you write a stronger essay with time to spare. We'll reveal which topics work best and the kind of research you need to do—all illustrated with in-depth examples.

Chapter 3 takes you through the all-important first five minutes of your essay. From determining heartbeat words to matching your content to the essay assignment and writing a thesis statement, each step is explained with plenty of examples. In Chapter 4, you'll put your knowledge to the test by completing five planning practice sessions, designed to help you get good—and fast—at planning essays.

In Chapter 5, we'll work our way through the essay, starting with the introduction. Learn what to include and how to start with a hook that will really catch your readers. Discover how to write body paragraphs that make the most of your examples, using the supporting evidence and details that scorers are looking for. Finally, you'll understand how to wrap it all up with a conclusion that leaves a strong final impression.

Chapters 6 and 7 are writer's workshops, lessons that will help you firm up your skills in all the areas SAT essay readers are trained to evaluate. From grammar to mechanics and word usage, it's all there.

Ready to test your knowledge and skills? Chapter 8 is comprised of five practice sessions, each ending with a self-guided assessment. Then, you'll be prompted to complete a second online essay (the first prompt is at the end of this Introduction) to get feedback on specific areas you may still need to improve. Want to check your results against other essays? Chapter 9 has six of them that vary in quality. Each is followed by a score and an analysis.

In the Appendix, we've included five additional practice sessions, a list of the top 50 SAT words, as well as a guide to the best print and online college admissions resources.

Write Your Way into College: Master the SAT Essay will teach you the right way:

- approaching the SAT essay like a math problem
- practicing in five minute sessions to plan better essays

- preparing much of your essay ahead of time
- locating and using heartbeat words to keep your essay focused
- coming up with examples that support your thesis

It will also teach you how to avoid the wrong way:

- wasting time by reading the directions and the prompt
- jumping into writing
- saving your best example for last
- telling rather than showing
- not practicing because you don't know what the specific assignment will be

Where Do You Stand Now?

A unique feature of *Write Your Way into College* is its two companion online practice SAT essays. These essays offer you the essential SAT essay writing practice you need, coupled with instant scoring to help you quickly identify areas of strength and weakness in your writing, to better focus your preparation.

Before you work your way through this book, you should complete the first online essay to see where you currently stand with your essay writing skills. To get started, simply log in to the LearningExpress website at www.learnatest.com/practice. See Additional Practice Online on page 165 for instructions on how to log in. Once logged in, you'll find two different practice SAT essays. Both of these online essays contain assignments similar to the type of writing assignment you'll find on the official SAT essay, and you will have a 25-minute timer to help you practice your time management. When you are ready to begin, choose the first essay.

About Your Online Essay Scores

Your official SAT essay will be scored holistically, meaning that the official graders will give you a single score between 1 and 6 based on their overall impression. The graders will look for six specific things in your writing, elements essential to every strong essay: organization, support, sentence structure, mechanics, grammar, and word choice.

Your practice online essays, however, are a little different—they will be scored diagnostically. What does this mean? When you complete an online practice essay, you'll instantly receive a report with not one, but six different scores between 1 and 6, in each of those writing elements evaluated by the official SAT essay graders. These separate scores are more helpful to you because they offer a diagnosis of the strengths and weaknesses in your writing to better target your preparation and practice.

Below is the scoring guide that will be used to grade your online practice essays. Study it well, as it offers you a good idea of what the six essential writing elements are and what it takes to demonstrate strength in each of these areas.

Scoring Guide

	Organization	Support	Sentence Structure	Grammar/ Word Choice	Mechanics
	• The degree to which the response is: (1) focused (2) clearly and logically organized	• The degree to which the response includes examples that develop the main points	• The degree to which the response includes sentences that are: (1) complete and correct (2) varied in structure and length	• Usage • Vocabulary • Word choice	• Spelling • Punctuation • Capitalization
Score: 6	• Fully and smoothly organized from beginning to end • Awareness of audience and task is evident throughout • Clear focus • Logical order • A seamless flow of ideas	• Fully developed • Supporting details are pertinent and thorough • Details are relevant to audience and focus • All points are well supported • Original, insightful	• Virtually no errors in structure or usage • Sentence variety enhances style and effect • Demonstrates command and control of more sentence constructions	• Correct usage with length and complexity • Precise, effective vocabulary • Fresh, vivid language	• Virtually no or no mechanical errors in a text that has length and complexity
Score: 5	• Organized from beginning to end • Clear awareness of audience and task • Focused, stays on topic • Logical order • Fluent	• Ideas developed in depth • Details are strong but lack specificity • Details are relevant to audience and focus • Most points are evenly supported • Solid	• Few or no errors in structure or usage • Sentence variety is appropriate to style and effect • May demonstrate command and control of more complicated sentence constructions	• Correct usage with length • Effective vocabulary • Generally successful in using vivid language	• Few or no mechanical errors in a text that has length and complexity

Score: 4	• Generally organized • Awareness of audience and task • Focused with minor lapses • Moderately fluent	• Ideas developed but limited in depth • Adequate to support the focus • Details are generally relevant to audience and focus • Support is a mixture of general and specific information	• Few errors in structure or usage • Some sentence variety • Attempts to use more complicated sentence constructions	• Generally correct usage • Acceptable vocabulary • Attempts to use vivid language • Correct usage but limited text	• Few mechanical errors • Limited text but mechanically correct
Score: 3	• Poor transitions • Some awareness of audience and task • Focus unclear or limited, strays from topic • Somewhat organized	• Thinly developed • Support lacks specificity • Some elaboration, does not support the focus • Repetitive	• Noticeable errors in structure or usage • Little sentence variety • Excessive reliance on simple or repetitive constructions	• Noticeable errors in usage • Simplistic vocabulary with limited word choice	• Noticeable mechanical errors • Errors are disproportionate to the length or complexity of the piece • Brief text but mechanically correct
Score: 2	• Thought patterns are difficult to follow • Poor awareness of audience and task • Unfocused • Lacks clarity • Little evidence of organzation	• Poorly developed • Little support • Repetitive	• Serious errors in structure or usage interfere with meaning • No sentence variety • Too brief to demonstrate variety	• Numerous errors in usage • Simplistic vocabulary with inappropriate and/or incorrect word choice • Too brief to demostrate variety	• Mechanical errors that interfere with communication • Errors are disproportionate to the length or complexity of the piece • Insufficient text but mechanically correct
Score: 1	• No organization, too short • No awareness of audience or task • Inappropriate response, off topic	• Not developed • Virtually no support • Irrelevant	• Riddled with errors • Lack of sentence sense • Too brief to evaluate	• Riddled with errors • Inadequate vocabulary • Too brief to evaluate	• Mechanical errors that seriously interfere with communication • Too brief to evaluate

Keep your score in mind as you read *Write Your Way into College*, paying careful attention to the area or areas that need work. At the end of Chapter 8, you'll be prompted to complete another online essay, and you'll be able to note where you've improved and where work is still needed.

About the Instant Essay Scoring Program

It is important to note that although the automated essay scoring system is extremely reliable, it does presume good faith effort, essays submitted by writers who wish to get reliable scores on their writing. Efforts to fool the system by typing in nonsense, repetitive phrases, or off-topic prose will definitely produce illogical results. You may get a score, but the result will be meaningless in helping you improve your writing skills.

WRITE YOUR WAY INTO COLLEGE

MASTER THE SAT ESSAY

1

YOUR
SAT ESSAY
QUESTIONS
ANSWERED

The SAT essay is unlike any other writing you've done to date. Even if you've taken an essay exam, it was most likely graded by a teacher who knows you and your work. On the SAT, you are completely anonymous to the people who will give your writing a score. Here, we answer some of the most frequently asked questions about the essay, providing an overview of everything you need to know. You'll learn the basics of the essay, including who scores your writing and what they're looking for, whether personal essays work, and how to budget your time.

Preparing for the SAT Essay

"The SAT Essay seems overwhelming! I'm not even sure how to start preparing for it."

While most students aren't thrilled at the prospect of completing 170 multiple-choice questions (the total on the SAT) in about three hours, they get even more nervous about writing in a timed test setting. Because you won't know what you'll be asked to write about until you get your test booklet, you might think there's very little you can do to prepare. The good news is that's wrong! In fact, there are four distinct steps you can take to help you conquer the SAT essay, and this book is divided into chapters that guide you through each one.

First, as with every other part of the SAT, you need to understand what you're required to do. What will you be asked to write about? What are scorers looking for? How do they determine your score? How much should you write?

Second, you should formulate a plan. Many students are surprised to learn that they can prepare most of their essay content well before the test—without knowing exactly what they'll be asked to write about. Decide on four topics and do some research. Be prepared to discuss each topic in terms of at least four themes.

The next step is to refine your essay writing skills. Scorers are taking note of your vocabulary and word choice, and although they won't take off points for a stray comma or random grammatical error, they are looking for evidence of mastery of the language. Because you already know the topics you'll be writing about, you can choose a few "wow" words that will impress your readers. You'll also want to review the most common grammar and mechanics errors so you can avoid them—these are the types of errors you'll also find in the SAT Writing multiple-choice sections, so learning them now will help you gain points there too.

Finally, you need to practice. We're not talking about writing essay after essay—since there's no one to score them for you, writing a bunch of complete essays isn't a valuable use of your time. But five-minute practice sessions are critical. Three or four times a week until your test date, choose a prompt, set the timer, and plan an essay based on your chosen topics. When your planning skills are honed, writing the complete essay is the easy part.

Your Goal: A Polished Rough Draft

"It takes me a week or more to write a good essay. How can I get one finished in 25 minutes?"

Here's the best news about the SAT essay: The College Board knows almost no student can create a great essay in 25 minutes. And they don't expect you to. Instead, they look for a polished rough draft. A couple of minor errors in grammar, usage, and mechanics will not be weighed against you. Neither will a few factual glitches (can't remember who bombed Pearl Harbor? Your history teacher isn't checking, and your readers won't hold it against you).

LEARN THE ESSAY DIRECTIONS—NOW!

SAT experts have calculated that it takes the average student about 12 minutes to read every set of directions on the SAT. That's 12 minutes you don't have to write your essay or answer multiple-choice questions. Weeks before the test, go to www.collegeboard.com and locate the directions for the essay and every type of question. Read the directions carefully and most importantly, make sure you understand them. You'll save valuable time that you can use to gain points.

Scorers read the essay to get an overall impression of your writing ability. They look for evidence of critical thinking, looking to see how well you do the following:

- develop a point of view using appropriate examples and evidence to support your position
- write with a clear focus, transitioning smoothly from one point to the next
- avoid errors in grammar, mechanics, and usage
- vary sentence structure
- show evidence of a varied and intelligent vocabulary

To get a high score, you'll need to hit each of the marks they're looking for. But perfection isn't the key to a high score.

Essay Scoring

"Who scores my essay and how are they judging my writing? Is it true that only long essays get a 5 or 6?"

SAT essays are scanned and distributed to scorers via the Internet. Two scorers, who are high school or college writing teachers, read each essay. They are trained to spend two to three minutes on each, considering it holistically. That means they're not reading it as one of your teachers would; a few minor errors in grammar or spelling won't count against you, nor will a few factual errors. They're reading for an overall impression, rather than to pick it apart.

Each reader assigns a score of 1–6 (although an essay that is written off topic gets a 0). A score of 1 shows writing incompetence while a 6 demonstrates clear and consistent competence. The two scores are then added, bringing the total to 2–12. If the graders disagree by more than a point, a third reader is brought in. The College Board reports that fewer than 5% of all essays require a third reader.

Although scores are based on a holistic impression, readers are trained to respond to certain key areas including: meaning (your ideas), development (how well you support your ideas), organization (how one idea flows to the next), and language use or mechanics (word choice, grammar, and punctuation). The College Board website has a detailed explanation of these areas and how they relate to each score.

When the SAT Writing section was introduced in 2005, it was met with plenty of skepticism. Many colleges announced that they would not consider scores from the new section until they had a chance to determine whether performance on this part of the test correlated with college-level writing ability. There was also some criticism. One MIT professor was, and remains today, particularly vocal in his opposition. He studied the essay examples that were made public and found that he was able to guess their scores simply by looking at how long they were (the longer the essay, the better the score).

The College Board responded that longer essays were generally more well written and developed than shorter ones but that length alone was not a scoring factor. However, if you check the sample essays in the College Board's Official Study Guide, you'll see that every 5 and 6 essay is more than one page. Use this information to your advantage. Whichever side you're on, the message is clear: Develop your point of view with at least three examples that you explore in separate paragraphs. Use details and evidence as support. Follow that advice, along with what you'll learn in Chapters 3 and 4, and you'll end up with an essay of at least one and a half pages.

THE RUMOR MILL

Because the SAT is such a high stakes test, and the process of creating and administering it is not completely transparent, it lends itself to rumors. One long-standing rumor says that a representative from a test prep company revealed that the computers that scan SAT essays are programmed to score those that are very short and/or are broken down into very few paragraphs anywhere from a 1 to a 3, *without the benefit of a human reader*. Whether it's true or false, this rumor highlights the very real fact that longer essays tend to get higher scores than shorter ones. When you develop your point of view and support it well with examples and evidence, you'll end up with a longer essay. You'll find more on that in Chapter 4.

The Directions

"Why should I know the directions ahead of time? Aren't they pretty straight-forward?"

You need to know the directions for the essay for the same reason you need to know them for every other part of the SAT. First, it saves valuable time. Again, you can gain about 12 minutes to answer more questions and write more sentences by skipping the directions—that's almost half the time allotted for a typical section of the SAT!

Second, being familiar with the test, being prepared, and knowing exactly what you'll be facing greatly reduces anxiety. There is no excuse for taking the SAT without knowing ahead of time how the test is structured, how each question type works, and what they're looking for. The more familiar you are, the less stress you'll feel. For the essay, that means not only getting right to work but being able to prepare much of what you'll write ahead of time. (Not a believer? Chapter 3 will explain exactly how it works!)

The official directions, which may be found at www.collegeboard.com/practice, direct you to use only the lines (two pages' worth) on your answer sheet and remind you to keep your handwriting legible. They also state that the essay is an opportunity for you to demonstrate how well you develop and express ideas. Your viewpoint should be logically developed, and you should take care to use language precisely.

The Prompt and Assignment

"What will I have to write about?"

Following the directions, you'll find a prompt, which is often a quote or a description of a situation. Prompts are usually a few sentences long, are adapted from books or articles, and present a clear point of view. Here's an example of an essay prompt:

There are only two kinds of choices available to us. First, the active: we make something happen and live with the consequences. Or we choose to not make a choice; we weigh the facts, decide the price of change is too high and make the choice to live with things as they are. The second kind of choice, the more dangerous, is the postponement of choice.

—Adapted from *Making Choices,* by ALEXANDRA STODDARD
(William Morrow and Company, 1994)

The assignment, which follows the prompt, tells you how to respond:

Can deciding to not make a choice be dangerous? Plan and write an essay in which you develop your point of view on this issue. Support your position with reasoning and examples taken from your reading, studies, experience, or observations.

Every assignment will ask you a question and then direct you to write your essay using examples that are academic, personal, or a blend of the two. In Chapter 2, you'll find more detailed information about types of prompts and assignments—and what to do first after you read them.

Every Essay Is a Persuasive Essay

"I've heard that SAT essay questions are pretty similar. Can you explain?"

While subjects may vary, every assignment asks you to take a stand or develop your point of view on an issue. That means you need to write a *persuasive* essay, one whose goal is to persuade the reader to accept your opinion. Persuasive essays use logic and reasoning to make their case; even when emotions are meant to be included, the writer has a specific reason for doing so. He or she expects those emotions to get the reader to accept the essay's viewpoint.

If you were writing a persuasive essay for a class, you would have time to do some research. Simply stating your case isn't enough. You need to support it with evidence, examples, facts, statistics, and even quotes from experts. But during the SAT, you won't have access to the Internet or any other research tool. That's one of the reasons it's so important to develop content ahead of time. In Chapter 3, you'll learn how to generate topics that will strengthen and support your point of view—no matter what the writing assignment.

WHAT DOESN'T WORK

Persuasive essays reveal firm opinions and are developed to persuade the reader of the validity of those opinions. Waffling (admitting you might be wrong or that the other side of the argument is just as valid) will weaken your argument. A confident tone and a viewpoint that's backed up with meaningful examples creates a high-scoring essay.

Budgeting Your Time

"I have a hard time answering all the multiple-choice questions in 25 minutes. How can I write an essay in such a short time?"

Twenty-five minutes can go by quickly without a plan. But knowing exactly how you'll spend this time—and practicing—before the test will help you make sure you use each minute to your advantage.

Spend the first four to six minutes *planning* your essay. Skipping this step can result in an essay that wanders, rather than one that logically develops a point of view. It can also lead you off topic (remember that the only way to get a 0 is to write an essay that fails to address the assignment). You'll want to write a thesis statement in which you take a stand on the assignment's question, and then come up with three ideas that help you develop your point of view.

The next 14–17 minutes will be spent *drafting* your essay. Chapter 4 provides detailed instruction for each paragraph, including sentence structure and word choice. Finally, use any remaining minutes to check your essay for missing words or grammar and mechanics errors.

The Fiction Factor

"I understand that a few factual errors won't count against me. But what if I deliberately make something up?"

Here's another important point to remember about your readers: They don't know you. Not only are they instructed not to deduct points for an incorrect date or a misspelled name, but they have no idea who your friends and family are. If you can't come up with a third example, you can simply make one up. Using the sample prompt and assignment on page 6, imagine that two of your predetermined topics worked well, but then you got stuck. You can do one of two things: Wrap up the (short) essay in four paragraphs, or come up with one more example. That example might be the fictitious situation of a friend or relative or something like this: "A recent story in *The New York Times* described a tragic situation in Iraq. A commanding officer was unsure of whether to advance his troops. While he tried to decide, his unit was ambushed." Is this true? No. Does it matter, or will it be counted against you? Again, no.

It's easier for most students to come up with a situation involving a friend or an older relative. Need an example of a bad decision? The friend who blew off studying for a big test to go to a party. Or the elderly uncle who quit his job to sell a "surefire" product door-to-door—right before the company that made the product went bankrupt.

Your score on the SAT essay is based on how well you develop and support your point of view—not on the accuracy or truth of the information you use.

There's an "I" in SAT Essay

"I've always been told to keep 'I' statements out of my essays. My teachers only want me to back up what I say with facts and expert opinion."

Here's another important difference between your classroom writing and the SAT: The College Board *encourages* you to use personal examples and evidence in your essay. The directions always state that your experiences and observations are fair game, and scorers are instructed not to deduct points for personal rather than academic content.

Your reader can't give you a score if he or she can't figure out what you've written. Unless your cursive is very easy to read, print your essay. The importance of legibility can't be overstated.

What the Essay Measures

"I know I can write a better essay when I'm not rushed or nervous. What can colleges learn about my writing ability from my SAT Essay score?"

Much of the controversy surrounding the SAT essay (and the Writing section in general) has to do with whether it's a true measure of your writing ability. The Writing section was developed in response to an outcry from colleges who were tired of admitting students who couldn't write well. They sought some way to determine writing ability within the admissions process. But is the College Board's answer really what they were looking for?

For most of your classes in college, you'll be given essay assignments and have a period of time in which to draft, edit, and rewrite your work. Occasionally, you'll also get essay exams. The SAT essay is obviously more like an exam than a take-home assignment. But the SAT also differs significantly from college essay exams. Your professor will be asking you to demonstrate how well you have learned the material that has been covered in his or her course. So even though you might not know the exact subject, your writing will be based on specific readings and lectures. The SAT essay assignments are completely unknown (although, as you'll see in Chapter 3, they're general enough that you can prepare content in advance that can address them).

So is your ability to write on an unknown topic in 25 minutes a true measure of your writing ability? The answer to that question is still up for debate.

2 CHOOSING AND RESEARCHING CONTENT

The College Board adamantly states that because the SAT essay deals with specific issues, you won't be able to prepare an essay ahead of time. But that's not quite true. It is precisely because of the issues the prompts address—ones that can be approached effectively from a number of different angles—that you can determine much of what you'll write before the test. So although you won't be able to walk into the SAT with a memorized essay, you will be able to enter with well-developed content that should need only minor work to address the prompt.

WORD OF WARNING

The College Board recently added a reminder to the essay practice section of their website which notes that if your essay is not "your original and individual work," they may cancel your scores. Be advised that this chapter uses examples to illustrate how you can prepare your own content for the essay. Using these examples when you take the test could be considered plagiarism and result in cancelled scores. Use the examples as guidelines, and use only your own work.

As you'll notice in the following examples—taken from literature, the visual arts, history, and science—the best topics have many different themes. Something very narrow, such as a specific sport, probably won't work for many prompts. But the topic of professional sports as a whole is complex enough to apply to a range of issues. Once you've chosen your topics, think in the broadest possible terms about angles through which you can discuss them. If you're prepared to write about your topics in a variety of ways, you'll be able to quickly link them to the assignment.

Essay topics preparation is much like learning mathematical proofs or formulas. Once you know your topics, you can take the test and apply them. The prompts will change, but the way you approach them will be consistent.

But don't stop your preparation with themes. In Chapter 1, you learned the importance of writing an essay of at least one and a half pages. You'll be able to do that easily if you develop two to four strong supporting sentences for each topic. These sentences will work no matter what the assignment and will stretch your essay to the right length while remaining on task.

Note that some topics lend themselves to a few additional areas of research. For novels, be certain you understand the main characters. For a historical event such as the Great Depression, it makes sense to think in terms of cause and effect. Because quotations add great impact to an introduction or conclusion, do some research and include one or two for each topic. They won't always work, but it makes sense to have them ready.

KEEP IN MIND

You're not writing a term paper for a class. Scorers, unlike teachers, are not looking for factual accuracy, so if you can't remember who wrote *Animal Farm* or the exact date of the bombing of Hiroshima, don't worry. You can either guess (points won't be deducted if you're wrong) or simply write about your topic without mentioning the author, date, or other piece of forgotten information.

Selecting Topics

Literature: Choose a book you know fairly well. Notice that many of the classics you're asked to read in high school are categorized as such because they contain universal themes. These themes don't go out of date or lose their relevance no matter how many decades or centuries have passed since they've been written. Examples include *The Catcher in the Rye*, *Of Mice and Men*, *Romeo and Juliet*, *Animal Farm*, *The Scarlet Letter*, and *Lord of the Flies.*

Arts and Music: While a description of a painting, sculpture, or concerto adds body and interest to your essay, it's the background and themes that will effectively answer the essay assignment. A composer such as Mozart; a specific work with an exciting, complex backstory like Picasso's *Guernica*; the history of body art; and the fate of the music industry are all subjects that have the depth and flexibility you're looking for.

History: If dozens of books have been written about an episode in history, you can safely assume that there are many angles from which to approach it. Conflicts such as World War II and the U.S. Revolution and Civil War are obvious choices, but other events can also work well. The Great Depression, Civil Rights Movement, and Watergate are complex and involve specific personalities, politics, and lessons that are relevant today. Know at least one historian's work that deals specifically or famously with the event you choose.

Science and Technology: Although you don't want to espouse ideas that many would consider radical, you don't need to worry about alienating your reader as you would if you were writing an application essay. That said, the best science and technology topics have ramifications in areas beyond science. Space travel, for example, can be discussed in terms of politics, ethics, and economics. Climate change, alternative energy sources, transportation, and gaming are other possibilities for science topics that lend themselves to multiple areas of discussion.

Historical Biography: Choose someone who has made her mark on history. Themes should include reasons for this person's importance, her relevance today, and qualities she exemplifies. (Was she known for honesty, perseverance, intelligence?) Be sure to include a couple of quotes that illustrate one or more of the themes you identify.

Sample Content

Below you will find sample content notes for each of the topics we just reviewed. When preparing your notes, your goal is to understand and explore the major themes of the topics you choose. You should develop basic background information in two to four sentences and reference characters, settings, and/or author as applicable. Note that the final topic (#6) represents your fictitious relative or friend who can be used to support any essay when a third example is needed.

KEEP IN MIND

Because one of the writing qualities your scorers will be looking for is variety in sentence structure, develop background information using at least one simple sentence and a longer one that is more complex.

1. Literature: Nathaniel Hawthorne's *The Scarlet Letter*

Background
The Scarlet Letter was written by Nathaniel Hawthorne in 1850. As a descendent of one of the judges of the Salem Witch Trials, Hawthorne was interested in America's Puritan past. He set *The Scarlet Letter* in seventeenth century Boston, where the strict moral code and intolerance for dissent of any kind have a profound impact on the characters in the novel.

Characters
Hester Prynne (Prynne rhymes with sin); Reverend Arthur Dimmesdale (the character is dim, weak, not able to comprehend well); Roger Chillingworth (brings a chill to Hester's, Pearl's, and Dimmesdale's lives); Pearl, Hester's daughter (in the Bible, salvation is described as the Pearl of Great Price).

Themes
A. Secrecy. Hester refuses to reveal the identity of her baby Pearl's father; Chillingworth finds a mysterious mark on Dimmesdale's chest that is not described for the reader until the end of the novel; psychological torment of Dimmesdale—is it because he is keeping a secret? Dimmesdale dies immediately after confessing publicly—revealing the secret that he is Pearl's father.

B. Sin and knowledge. Goes back to the Garden of Eden, where Adam and Eve sin by eating the forbidden fruit from the tree of the knowledge of good and evil. They are then thrown out of the garden. Hester and Dimmesdale sin and are cast out of their community. They experience suffering and gain greater knowledge about the human condition because of that sin. Dimmesdale is a more compassionate person and preacher because he has fallen. Hester leads a life on the fringes of society but does good work to help those less fortunate than herself.

C. Evil. Who or what is truly evil? There is debate within the novel about the identity of the "Black Man" (evil). Hester and Dimmesdale's relationship (sin) is not described as evil but Chillingworth's vengeance is. Pearl says it is evil that Dimmesdale will not own up to being her father in public. He withholds his love from his own child.

D. Identity. Hester: Boston society, by making her wear the Scarlet Letter, is imposing an identity on Hester. But Hester refuses to be limited by it and even claims it as her own. She won't move away (where she would not be known as an adulterer or have to wear the A) and even gets upset when Chillingworth tells her she might be able to remove the letter. The Native Americans who see her at the end of the novel think it is the symbol of an important person. Dimmesdale: His role as minister means people don't see him as a regular person. The role both defines and limits him. Pearl: She is the result of Hester and Dimmesdale's sin, but she is also a great blessing to her mother's life, giving Hester a reason to continue when all of society has pushed her away.

Key Quotes

> "We are not, Hester, the worst sinners in the world. There is one worse than even the polluted priest! That old man's revenge has been blacker than my sin."

> "No man, for any considerable period, can wear one face to himself, and another to the multitude, without finally getting bewildered as to which may be true."

2. Art: Picasso's *Guernica*

Background
In 1937, Pablo Picasso painted a mural for the World's Fair in Paris. It depicts the aftermath of the German bombing of Guernica, a city in his native Spain.

Themes
A. Art as a political protest or statement. Picasso never painted a politically themed picture before and often said that he did not believe art should be

used as a political statement. However, the bombing in his native country was so devastating that he changed his mind.

B. Hope. Even in the darkest times, there is still hope (the painting includes a lightbulb within a sun shape and a flower held in the hand of a victim). The belief that things will get better helps people who are suffering to keep going.

C. War as unheroic and brutal. This represents a break with art of the past that glorified the violence and sacrifice of battle. Innocent victims include animals (a horse and a bull are pictured).

D. Use of color. Black, white, and gray give the painting the look of a newspaper and represent violence as abstract rather than realistic. Picasso learned of the massacre through eyewitness accounts and photographs in the newspapers of Paris, where he was living at the time.

E. Indecision. By waiting to choose a theme, Picasso was presented with a terrible event that proved to be a powerful subject for his painting.

Key Quote

> "Art is the lie that enables us to realize the truth."

3. History: The Great Depression

Background
On October 29, 1929, the United States stock market crashed. This event, along with bank failures, consumers' fears that kept them from making purchases, bad governmental policies, and even the environment came together to create a worldwide economic collapse. Recovery would take nearly a decade.

Themes
A. Excess of the 1920s. Hundreds of thousands of Americans bought stock—many even borrowing money to do so. Share prices rose, creating an economic bubble. One economist echoed the sentiments of many when he said the market had reached a "permanently high plateau." The bubble burst on October 29, 1929, when over 16 million shares were traded, and the stock market lost about 12% of its value (added to the 13% lost the day before).

B. Fear. People lost confidence as they watched the markets plunge. This led to dramatically reduced spending and a run on the banks. Fewer goods purchased meant less production and a decrease in the workforce (25+% unemployment). Massive withdrawals plus defaults on loans led to the failure of almost half of all U.S. banks.

C. Protectionism. The Smoot-Hawley Act tried to protect the American economy by heavily taxing imports. This led to less trade with other countries as well as retaliatory policies of former trading partners. In today's global economy, such policies are even more foolhardy and can lead to devastating consequences.

D. Action versus inaction. Britain and Japan moved quickly to leave the gold standard, meaning their currency could no longer be exchanged for gold. As a result, the economies of these countries recovered more quickly than those that waited to leave the gold standard (including the United States, France, and Italy). This cause and effect relationship is explained in Economist Barry Eichengreen's book *Golden Fetters: The Gold Standard and the Great Depression* (1992).

E. Environment. Drought plus farming practices that damaged soil caused the Dust Bowl. Livestock, crops, and machinery were destroyed, and more people were put out of work. About 800,000 so-called Okies moved to California looking for jobs (John Steinbeck's *The Grapes of Wrath* deals with this).

Outcomes
Rise of extremism in Germany leads to election of Adolf Hitler; election of Franklin Delano Roosevelt over Herbert Hoover brings New Deal in America; Smoot-Hawley policy eroded trust and cooperation between nations.

Key Quotes

"Brother, can you spare a dime?"
(refrain from a popular song from 1931)

". . . the only thing we have to fear is fear itself."
(President FRANKLIN DELANO ROOSEVELT)

4. Science: Climate Change

Background
The Earth has become about one degree (Fahrenheit) warmer in the last century. No one is debating that fact, but there is considerable debate about why this warming is happening and how, if at all, we can stop it.

Themes
A. Science. Greenhouse effect—use of fossil fuels and electricity is tied to warming temperatures.

B. Political. Countries that support this view are joining together to try to combat it. Kyoto Protocol of 1997 (came into effect in 2005) is a legally binding agreement of 186 countries to reduce greenhouse gas emissions.

C. Economics. Cost benefit analysis: Is the price of compliance to reduce greenhouse gas emissions cost-effective? Should taxes be put on fuels in proportion to their carbon dioxide content?

D. Agriculture. Agriculture is very vulnerable to climate change. This could challenge countries whose GDP is dependent on agriculture; may be harder to produce enough food for the world population.

E. Technology. How can we get energy without emitting greenhouses gases? There is an effort to find/make alternative, nonpolluting energy sources; clean coal is being explored, as well as geo-engineering solutions, such as increasing cloud formations and the amount of CO_2 absorbed by oceans.

Key Quotes

> "The danger posed by war to all of humanity—and to our planet—is at least matched by the climate crisis and global warming."
> (UN Secretary General BAN KI-MOON)

> "Few challenges facing America—and the world—are more urgent than combating climate change."
> (President BARACK OBAMA)

5. Historical Biography: Thomas Edison

Background

American inventor Thomas Edison (1847–1931) has been described as more responsible than anyone else for creating the modern world. In his research laboratory in Menlo Park, New Jersey, he invented the phonograph, made the electric lightbulb, and started the motion picture industry.

CONSIDER THIS

Because about 20% of SAT essay assignments to date have had something to do with emotions and/or the reason for certain behaviors, develop a corresponding theme for each of your content topics. Consider Edison's relationship with his mother, for example, or the fear that helped to worsen the Great Depression. These kinds of themes will help make your content more flexible and adaptable to a wide range of assignments.

Themes

A. Perseverance. Not all of Edison's inventions were successful. Although he had over 1,000 patents, he had some ideas that never took off such as using cement to build phonographs, pianos, and buildings. Edison's greatest failure was an attempt to invent a practical way to mine iron ore. He lost a fortune in the attempt. But he did not stop inventing and built the largest laboratory in existence in 1886. More than half of his inventions began in that laboratory.

B. Lack of formal education. Edison spent only a few months at school. He constantly questioned everything, and this upset his teacher who said he was slow. His mother became so angry that she withdrew him from school after just three months and taught him at home.

C. Early "green" pioneer. Edison developed the alkaline battery for use in cars, but by the time he perfected it, electric cars were being replaced by gasoline powered ones. The battery had many other uses, though, and was very profitable.

D. Cooperation between scientists and the military. Edison headed the Naval Consulting Board before and during World War I. The board brought together scientists and inventors to aid the military.

Key Quotes

"Genius is 1% inspiration and 99% perspiration."

"I have not failed. I've just found 10,000 ways that won't work."

"My mother was the making of me. She was so true, so sure of me."

6. Personal

Background

High-school-aged friend, male or female, who conveniently illustrates the necessary theme or an older relative who serves the same purpose.

Themes

Any

Researching Your Content

Now, it's your turn. While it's perfectly acceptable to research four to six topics that are new to you, it makes more sense to choose ones that you already have some knowledge of. The more you bring to these topics and the more broadly you can think about them, the easier it will be to adapt them to a specific essay prompt.

For each background section, aim for two to four sentences that set the scene for your topic. Show off your knowledge and prepare the reader by giving some general information before making the connection with the essay assignment.

It is important to practice writing up your notes as you research a topic. The better you are at this, the more time you will save during the exam. Adequate preparation will also ensure that your essay is well organized, includes themes that are easily identifiable by the scorer, and has enough supporting information to achieve the highest possible score.

Hamlet / Aeneid

Bach Cello Suites

Francois

Battle of Monmouth

Mary Sherman Morgan / Virginia Hall

Karate - personal experience

Topic 1 The Aeneid

Background Vergil wrote the Aeneid in
31 CE to tell the long history
of the founder of Rome.

Themes loyalty

unusual hero

— categories —

Authority/heroes, Success, Past v. Present,

Behaviors + Emotions, Learning.

Quote(s) "and perhaps someday it will
please us to remember these things"
forsan et olim meminisse...

Topic 2 _Hamlet_

Background _Written by William Shakespeare in 1596, Hamlet tells the story of a prince who's downfall is his indecision._

Themes _Choices/Problem Solving, Learning, Authority/Heroes, Individuality v. Groups, Success_

Quote(s) _"Neither a borrower nor a lender be." "The play's the thing wherein I'll catch the concience of the king"_

Topic 3 Pride and Prejudice

Background Written by Jane Austen in (first impression) 1813, Pride and Prejudice explores the new concept of marrying for love.

Themes Individuality v. Groups, Authority/Heroes, Modern Society? Past v. Present, Behaviors + Emotions, Choice/Problem Solving.

Quote(s)

Topic 4 To Kill a Mockingbird

Background Written by Harper Lee in 1963, To Kill a Mockingbird tackles the issue of racism and prejudice.

Themes Individuality v. Groups, Choices/Problem solving, Past v. Present, Learning.

Quote(s) You never really know someone until you get into their skin and walk around in it.

Topic 5 Morgan

Background

Themes – Oblivion

– Modesty   – Camera-shy

– impact   – change – innovation

– determination – thoughtfulness
– being careful.

Quote(s) from the play

Hall "My Neck is my own" – bravery

Topic 6 _Karate_

Background _I have been doing karate for eleven years._

Themes • Not Giving up
• Self-defense
• Courage • Integrity • Sportsmanship

Quote(s) What's wrong with being a martial artist?

3

UNDERSTANDING AND RESPONDING TO PROMPTS AND ASSIGNMENTS

Every SAT essay begins with a prompt, a short paragraph excerpted from a book, essay, or article. The essay prompt expresses a clear point of view on an issue. It's followed by an assignment that directs your writing. Most often, the assignment asks whether you agree or disagree with the prompt's position. The assignment also reminds you to back up your viewpoint with facts and examples from your classwork and reading (academic evidence) and/or what you have experienced or observed (personal evidence). You may choose to write a completely academic or personal essay, or combine the two.

SAT essay scorers are instructed to weigh academic and personal evidence equally. In fact, some of the examples on the College Board's website of the highest scoring essays are based completely on personal experience. So don't feel that your essay has to be solely academic to earn a high score.

Here's an example of an essay prompt:

There are only two kinds of choices available to us. First, the active: we make something happen and live with the consequences. Or we choose to not make a choice; we weigh the facts, decide the price of change is too high and make the choice to live with things as they are. The second kind of choice, the more dangerous, is the postponement of choice.

—Adapted from *Making Choices*, by ALEXANDRA STODDARD
(William Morrow and Company, 1994)

Here is the assignment for this prompt:

Can it be dangerous to postpone choices? Organize and compose an essay that establishes your viewpoint on this issue. Substantiate it with examples and evidence derived from what you have read, studied, experienced, or observed.

The Assignment Holds the Key

Looking carefully at the prompt and assignment, you'll notice that the prompt contains much more information than the assignment directs you to respond to. Specifically, the prompt introduces the idea that there are only two available choices, and then discusses how choices are made and the consequences that follow a choice. The assignment zeros in on one small part of the prompt—whether or not it's dangerous to postpone making a choice.

If you pay too much attention to the prompt or to any piece of information it contains rather than focusing on the assignment, you could easily write an essay that's off topic. (Recall that no matter how well written, an off-topic essay will receive a score of zero.) Therefore, it's critically important that you respond *exclusively* to the assignment as you plan your essay by choosing supporting information, and then writing a thesis statement.

Prompt:
People with great projects underfoot habitually look further and more clearly into the future than people who are mired in day-to-day concerns. These former control the future because by necessity they must project themselves into it. They are seldom intimidated by the alarms and confusions of the present

because they have something greater of their own, some sense of their large and coherent motion in time to compare the present with.

—Adapted from *Time and the Art of Living*, by ROBERT GRUDIN (Harper & Row, 1982)

Assignment:

Does having a plan for your future help keep the concerns of daily living in better perspective? Organize and compose an essay that establishes your viewpoint on this issue. Substantiate it with examples and evidence derived from what you have read, studied, experienced, or observed.

Notice again how the assignment gives you everything you need to write the essay, and the prompt gives much more information. In fact, it might take you two or three minutes to read the prompt and understand it. For this reason, it makes sense to *read the assignment first*. If you feel you need more information, check the prompt. But keep in mind that you must respond only to the assignment. Reading the prompt is *optional*; it takes valuable minutes you could have spent planning or writing and should only be done—if at all—after you've read the assignment.

Step One: Determining the Heartbeat Words

It's worth repeating (and repeating, and repeating): Your essay won't score any points, no matter how well written, if it's off topic. That means your very first goal in the seconds after you open your SAT test booklet is to read the essay assignment and understand exactly what it says. While the assignment almost always begins with a question asking whether you agree or disagree with the point of view of the prompt, you should *not* answer it at this stage.

The first question you should answer, no matter the assignment, is: What is the essential idea, and what word or words express it? Because those words are vital to your understanding of the assignment, and because repeating them throughout your essay—like a pulse—shows your reader that you're staying on topic, we'll call them the "heartbeat words." In the first example, the heartbeat words are *dangerous* and *choice*. In the second, *plan* and *perspective* are the words you're looking for.

More Examples

Review each of the assignment questions that follow. The italicized words show the heartbeat terms.

Do people truly *benefit* from *hardship* and *misfortune*?

Is it more *valuable* for people to *fit in* than to be unique and different?

Do people place too much *emphasis* on *winning*?

Can a group of people *function* effectively without someone being *in charge*?

Is it always *better* to be *original* than to imitate or use the ideas of others?

Exercise

Identify and circle the heartbeat words for each of the following five prompts. When in doubt, choose more words than fewer.

1. Should we admire heroes but not celebrities?
2. Are people more likely to be productive and successful when they ignore the opinions of others?
3. Has today's abundance of information only made it more difficult for us to understand the world around us?
4. Can knowledge be a burden rather than a benefit?
5. Is identity something people are born with or given, or is it something people create for themselves?

Answers

Note that circling more words than are necessary is okay, but there should generally be no more than three for each assignment. The answers are indicated here in italics.

1. Should we *admire heroes* but not *celebrities*?
2. Are people more likely to be *productive* and successful when they *ignore* the *opinions* of others?
3. Has today's abundance of *information* only made it more difficult for us to *understand* the world around us?
4. Can *knowledge* be a *burden* rather than a benefit?
5. Is *identity* something people are *born with* or given, or is it something people *create* for themselves?

Step Two: Matching Theme to Content

Once you've identified the heartbeat word or words, you'll need to consider the content notes you developed in Chapter 2. Using the first example, ask, "In what topics (literature, science and technology, history, arts and music, historical biography) does the theme of choice appear?" Think through your content carefully to find examples. Don't worry about matching them exactly to the assignment (whether postponing a choice is dangerous)—right now, you're only looking for a link to the essential idea of the assignment.

From the sample content in Chapter 2, here's what could work:

- *The Scarlet Letter*: Most characters have to make choices within the novel, including Dimmesdale's choice to refuse to acknowledge Pearl as his child until the end of the book.
- *Guernica*: Picasso's difficulty choosing a subject for his painting created a situation in which he became inspired by a massacre in the Spanish city of Guernica.
- The Great Depression: The U.S. government's decision to enforce the Smoot-Hawley Act is believed by many to have worsened the Depression because it reduced trade and led to retaliatory measures by other countries.
- Climate change: With the Kyoto Protocol, many countries are choosing to work together to reduce greenhouse gas emissions and develop alternative sources of energy.
- Thomas Edison: Although Edison had many setbacks and failures, including losing a fortune in a failed attempt to invent a practical way to mine iron ore, he chose to persevere, experimenting and inventing many useful things.

Notice that there is a link between *every* topic and the idea of choice. You might not be able to find as many links for every assignment, but two or three are enough to plan your essay. Once you've got a list of potential topics, you'll need to get more specific. Ask, "Is the idea of the danger of postponing a choice in any of these topics?" It's this question that will help you give a direct answer to the assignment. If there are three good examples in which postponing a choice is dangerous, these are the topics you should use in your essay.

Let's look at each example to find evidence of the postponement of a choice.

The Scarlet Letter: Dimmesdale chooses to keep secret the fact that he is Pearl's father, but he reveals it at the end of the novel. You could say, then, that he *postpones the choice* of revealing the truth. What are the consequences of that postponement? It means that he withheld his love from his child. Pearl calls him a "strange, sad man," and the weight of his secret takes an enormous toll on him both spiritually and physically. Once he reveals it, he dies.

Guernica: Picasso postponed making a choice, but what were the consequences? While he was waiting to decide on a subject for his mural, one presented itself to him. In response, he created *Guernica*, which is considered one of the most powerful antiwar statements in the history of art. This example won't work with the thesis statement.

The Great Depression: The Smoot-Hawley Act was a choice, but it wasn't postponed. But is there another theme within the topic of the Great Depression about postponement? Was the Depression worsened or lengthened because of some delay? In 1931, Britain and Japan left the gold standard, meaning they would no longer exchange their currency for gold. Both countries recovered from the Depression much more quickly than those that postponed suspending gold convertibility. The United States waited until 1933, and France and Italy did not drop the gold standard until 1936. Most economists agree that the delay in leaving the standard had a direct link to the length of a country's economic depression.

Climate change: The choice of countries to work together to reduce greenhouse gas emissions may be seen as a positive step toward protecting the earth from the potential disasters of climate change. But what about the countries that did not sign on and ratify the Kyoto Protocol? It could be said that the delay in taking action against global warming may contribute to more rapid negative consequences of climate change.

Thomas Edison: Edison is famous for saying that genius is 1% inspiration and 99% perspiration. But the inventor's postponement of calling off some of his experiments caused serious consequences for him. In 1890, he began seeking a more practical way to mine iron ore, which was needed by the steel mills in Pennsylvania. There was great demand, and Edison knew that if he could find a way to better supply the iron ore, it would bring financial success. He invested all of his stock in General Electric (the profit he made on his invention of the lightbulb). But after building a plant to process the ore and investing years of his life as well as part of his fortune, the venture was deemed a failure. Who knows what Edison could have done with the time and money he spent on this failed venture, in which he invested about 20 years of his life.

ASSIGNMENTS ABOUT CONTEMPORARY LIFE

You may get a question about an aspect of modern society: whether people have become more materialistic or whether today's youth are less willing to conform, for example. You don't necessarily need to abandon your developed content to address these assignments. An effective approach is to use examples from the past (whether biography, literature, or history) and disagree with the prompt.

Let's use the second example: Are youth less willing to conform today? To answer no would involve a thesis statement such as: Throughout history, youth have been unwilling to conform easily to society's expectations. (Note the heartbeat words *youth* and *conform*.) By taking this position, you don't have to say much about today's youth—you can simply show through detailed example evidence that youth have always resisted conformity. Hester Prynne was a young woman when she had an affair with Arthur Dimmesdale. She did so knowing the risk of such an act in her Puritanical Boston society. Likewise, Edison did not conform to the behaviors expected of him in school. His mother wisely removed him from the environment (encouraging his nonconformity in the 1800s!) and homeschooled him.

This approach can work for almost any modern society–themed assignment. Remember, it doesn't matter whether you actually agree or disagree. You simply need to choose a side and support it with appropriate examples.

Exercise

The second sample assignment has to do with *planning* and *perspective*. Using the topics introduced in Chapter 2, ask: *In what topics does the idea of planning appear? In what topics does planning lead to better perspective?* Aim to link each topic to these two questions.

Topic 1   Aeneas has to plan ahead for the survival of his people. He can not dwell on the negatives of the present. He's planning to the future leads to better perspective.

Topic 2   When working on the suites, I have to plan ahead what I want this piece to sound like. This will determine what bowings, fingerings, and phrasings I will use. Planning the overall future of the sound of the piece creates a goal for me to work to achieve.

Topic 3   Francois has planned to study with Edward Nanny—a great bassist. However he was unable to because Nanny had died 2 years before Francis ~~that~~ travelled to Paris to study with him.

Topic 4 General Lee planned to distract the Union Army and lead them away from Richmond by sending a force to the North (Maryland). This planning led to a better perspective of the needs of the whole Confederate army.

Topic 5 Morgan planned to discover which of the fuels already in use could be used to launch America's first satellite. Morgan planned for the end result (a fuel that works) and found a better perspective in that she had to invent a new one.

When you've finished, check your ideas against the following:

> *The Scarlet Letter*: Hester Prynne's daughter Pearl, like most children to their parents, is a symbol of the future. Although Hester's life as an outcast is difficult, her role as Pearl's mother gives her something to live for. Hester creates a life for herself and her daughter on the fringes of society and comes to accept her position. Even when Chillingworth tells her that she could leave and start a new life elsewhere, she chooses to stay.

Guernica: The feeling of hope may be interpreted as a plan for the future. When someone hopes, they believe that something better is coming, and they are able to endure the present. In Picasso's painting *Guernica*, the artist placed a flower and a lightbulb with sunlike rays around it in the midst of the devastations of war. These two symbols point to the <u>future</u> and help to lessen the pain of the present. With the bulb and the flower, Picasso was saying that things would get better.

The Great Depression: When the United States and much of the world's economies suffered a recession beginning in 2008, it was the lessons of the Great Depression that many experts turned to. Having that past example was important, and it helped to make people aware that we could take action.

Climate change: Many countries are planning ways to reduce the human contribution to global warming. These efforts include reducing greenhouse gas emissions and searching for cleaner forms of energy. It would be very easy to get depressed about the negative effects of climate change already being reported, such as the reduction in the size of polar ice caps. But knowing that great efforts are being made to lessen these effects helps to put the negative news in perspective.

Thomas Edison: Edison planned for the future by investing money in the largest laboratory in existence in 1886—knowing he would continue to try and invent useful things. This plan helped him to deal with the failures he experienced, such as a very expensive attempt to find a practical way to mine iron ore.

Notice that for each topic, a clear link is made between the idea of planning for the future and how such planning helps to give a better perspective on the present. Getting better at making these links comes with practice. You'll find five-minute exercises in Chapter 5 designed to improve your ability to think creatively about your topics and quickly create links to various assignments.

Step Three: Taking a Stand

You've got your list of links to the assignment. Now it's time to respond. Recall that most often you'll have the choice of agreeing or disagreeing with the point of view of the prompt. As you scan your list of links, an answer should be obvious. *Can it be dangerous to postpone choices?* For this assignment, check the links created with the topics from Chapter 2. There are a number of topics that can be used as examples, and it could be argued that the consequences of postponing choices can dangerous in some of the examples.

Since you only need two or three examples for your essay, it is during this step that you'll weigh the strength of each and choose your best material. In this case, the Picasso and Edison links to the assignment are the weakest. *The Scarlet Letter*, climate change, and the Great Depression topics provide the best examples of the dangers of postponing a choice.

TAKING A STAND THE RIGHT WAY

Do you agree or disagree with the question posed in the assignment? Many students make this their first step. Big mistake! You're not trying to decide whether you *actually* agree or disagree—your scorers don't know you and aren't concerned with how you think or feel about a given issue. Instead, develop a list of potential examples. Which side is supported by the majority of examples? That's the side you'll want to choose.

With that information, it's easy to answer the question in the assignment. Since three of the examples indicate that it can be dangerous to postpone a choice, the answer is yes. That answer becomes the basis for a thesis statement:

Postponing choices can not only lead to negative consequences, but those consequences can be dangerous.

Notice that this statement contains the heartbeat words *dangerous* and *choices,* and answers the question posed in the assignment.

Exercise

Now it's your turn. Using the list of examples for the second sample assignment (*planning* and *perspective*), complete these steps:

1. Choose the three examples that most strongly respond to the questions. (*In what topics does the idea of planning appear? In what topics does planning lead to better perspective?*)
2. Answer the assignment question. (*Does having a plan for your future help keep the concerns of daily living in better perspective?*)
3. Write a thesis statement that answers the assignment question using the heartbeat words *planning* and *perspective*.

1. Best examples The Aeneid → Romans plan for the Venus.

Hamlet → Catch the King.

P+P → Marriage to keep/get $

Me → bass playing setting 3-terms of goal,

TKMB →

2. Yes or no: *Does having a plan for your future help keep the concerns of daily living in better perspective?*

Yes

3. Thesis statement (using heartbeat words *planning* and *perspective*)

By planning for the future

While planning for the future can
~~seem~~ be tedious, it results in a better
perspective for daily living.

Reviewing Assignments by Theme

Since the SAT essay was introduced, there have been nearly 100 prompts and assignments. They can be grouped into nine themes: **Individuality versus Groups, Authority/Heroes, Creativity/Originality, Success, Modern Society, Choices/Problem Solving, Past versus Present, Behaviors and Emotions,** and **Learning.** Following, you'll find the assignments paraphrased and grouped within these themes.

Individuality versus Groups

Do people need to compare themselves with others to appreciate what they have? Yes, Arnold (fate) Francois "play like you" wrong

Are widely held views likely to be correct or are they often wrong? Francois
Morgan/hall Karate example - 3 people right 2 wrong.
Is there any value in belonging only to groups with which we have something in common? No

Is it necessary for people to combine their efforts with those of others in order to be most effective? Yes

Are organizations or groups most successful when their members pursue individual wishes and goals? No

Monocacy,

Is it always best to determine one's own views of right and wrong, or can we benefit from following the crowd? *Francois, Virginia Hall*

Do society and other people benefit when individuals pursue their own goals?

Is it more valuable for people to fit in than to be unique and different? *V. Hall, FR   Karate = Weapons @ tournament.*

Are people more likely to be productive and successful when they ignore the opinions of others? *No, constructive criticism learn from their opinions even if you disagree. Monocracy Karate*

Do we put too much value on the ideas or actions of individual people?

Authority/Heroes

Should we pay more attention to people who are older and more experienced than we are? *Yes learn from them but do not follow them blindly. FR*

Can a group of people function effectively without someone being in charge? *No, Aeneid Monocracy*

Is it important to question the ideas and decisions of people in positions of authority? *Yes FR*

Should *we* society limit people's exposure to some kinds of information or forms of expression? *Should we have censureship?,*

Do we benefit from learning about the flaws of people we admire and respect?

Are people's actions motivated primarily by a desire for power over others?

Should we limit our use of the term *courage* to describe people who risk their own well-being for the sake of others or to uphold a value?

Should we admire heroes but not celebrities? *Yes*

Is there a value in celebrating certain individuals as heroes?

Does fame bring happiness, or are people who are not famous more likely to be happy?

Creativity/Originality

Is it always better to be original than to imitate or use the ideas of others?

Is it better for a society when people act as individuals rather than copying the ideas and opinions of others?

Is creativity needed more than ever in the world today?

Do people achieve greatness only by finding out what they are especially good at and developing that attribute above all else?

Can people ever be truly original?

Does planning interfere with creativity?

Success

Do people truly benefit from hardship and misfortune?

Do people place too much emphasis on winning?

Does being ethical make it hard to be successful?

Is persistence more important than ability in determining a person's success?

Is the effort involved in pursuing any goal valuable, even if the goal is not reached?

Is it more important to do work that one finds fulfilling or work that pays well?

Do people achieve more success by cooperation than by competition?

Is it best for people to accept who they are and what they have, or should people always strive to better themselves?

Do success and happiness depend on the choices people make rather than on factors beyond their control?

Is criticism—judging or finding fault with the ideas and actions of others— essential for personal well-being and social progress?

Do highly accomplished people achieve more than others mainly because they expect more of themselves?

Can people achieve success only if they aim to be perfect?

Is it best to have low expectations and to set goals we are sure of achieving?

Modern Society

Does a strong commitment to technological progress cause a society to neglect other values, such as education and the protection of the environment?

Are there benefits to be gained from avoiding the use of modern technology, even when using it would make life easier?

Has today's abundance of information only made it more difficult for us to understand the world around us?

Is the most important purpose of technology today different from what it was in the past?

Have modern advancements truly improved the quality of people's lives?

Do newspapers, magazines, television, radio, movies, the Internet, and other media determine what is important to most people?

Should modern society be criticized for being materialistic?

Should people give up their privacy in exchange for convenience or free services?

Are the values of a society most clearly revealed in its popular culture?

Is it easier now to form friendships than ever before?

Choices/Problem Solving

Should people choose one of two opposing sides of an issue, or is the truth usually found in the middle?

Are decisions made quickly just as good as decisions made slowly and carefully?

Should people change their decisions when circumstances change, or is it best for them to stick with their original decisions?

Should people let their feelings guide them when they make important decisions?

Does having a large number of options to choose from make people happy?

Is using humor the best way to approach difficult situations and problems?

Is compromise always the best way to resolve a conflict?

Is it always necessary to find new solutions to problems?

Should people take more responsibility for solving problems that affect their communities or the nation in general?

Past versus Present

Do all established traditions deserve to remain in existence?

Do people need to unlearn, or reject, many of their assumptions and ideas?

Should people always prefer new things, ideas, or values to those of the past?

Do incidents from the past continue to influence the present?

Do memories hinder or help people in their efforts to learn from the past and succeed in the present?

Behaviors and Emotions

Should people always be loyal?

Do circumstances determine whether or not we should tell the truth?

Can deception—pretending that something is true when it is not—sometimes have good results?

Is it sometimes necessary to be impolite?

Is acting an essential part of everyday life?

Is identity something people are born with or given, or is it something people create for themselves?

Are people more likely to be happy if they focus on goals other than their own happiness?

Can people have too much enthusiasm?

Is it better to change one's attitude than to change one's circumstances?

Does everyone, even people who choose to live alone, need a network or family?

Learning

Do people put too much emphasis on learning practical skills?

Is the main value of the arts to teach us about the world around us?

Can books and stories about characters and events that are not real teach us anything useful?

Do images and impressions have too much of an effect on people?

Can common sense be trusted and accepted, or should it be questioned?

Does true learning only occur when we experience difficulties?

Is education primarily the result of influences other than school?

Should schools help students understand moral choices and social issues?

Should society limit people's exposure to some kinds of information or forms of expression?

Do we really benefit from every event or experience in some way?

Are all important discoveries the result of focusing on one subject?

Can knowledge be a burden rather than a benefit?

Do people learn more from losing than from winning?

4 THE FIVE-MINUTE PRACTICE SESSION

s you've learned, the first few minutes of the SAT Essay are critical. If you simply read the directions, the prompt, and the assignment, and then jump into writing, you're taking an enormous risk. You're counting on the fact that ideas will come to you as you write—ideas that are not only organized, but transition well from one to another.

Most writers can't pull that off. Instead, start with a plan that you've practiced often enough to feel confident that it will work. That plan includes three steps:

1. Determine the heartbeat word(s) and theme.
2. Match the theme to your pre-developed content.
3. Take a stand (choose your best examples and write a thesis statement).

In this chapter, you'll hone your planning ability by completing five separate exercises. But they're not meant to be done in one sitting. In fact, they're more effective if you do one per day. For each prompt and assignment, set a timer for five minutes and plan an essay using the three-step method.

When you're finished, evaluate your plan using the self-guided assessment at the end of each exercise, taking note of what worked—and what didn't. You may find that a content topic needs greater research and development or that you need more practice using your own experiences and observations (whether real or fictitious). These practice sessions will not only help you improve your planning skills, but they'll give you more confidence. The more times you attempt an SAT Essay prompt and assignment, the easier the experience will become.

Planning Session One

Prompt:

> *For the last half-century psychology has been consumed with a single topic only—mental illness—and has done fairly well with it. Psychologists can now measure such once-fuzzy concepts as depression and schizophrenia with considerable precision. But this progress has come at a high cost. Relieving the states that make life miserable has made building the states that make life worth living less of a priority. The time has arrived for a science that seeks to understand positive emotion and provide guideposts for what Aristotle called "the good life."*

> —Adapted from *Authentic Happiness*,
> by MARTIN SELIGMAN (Simon & Schuster, 2002)

Assignment:

> *Should happiness be humankind's primary goal? Organize and compose an essay that establishes your viewpoint on this issue. Substantiate it with examples and evidence derived from what you have read, studied, experienced, or observed.*

Heartbeat word(s) _"happiness" "goal"_

Match theme to content (In what topics does the theme of happiness appear? Is the idea of happiness the primary goal in any of these topics?)

Aeneid → remembering bad things could bring happiness.

Hamlet →

Pride + Prejudice → marriage for happiness not for wealth.

TKMB →

Thesis statement

The pursuit of happiness should be mankind's primary goal.

Best examples

• Pride and Prejudice →
Elizabeth Bennet believes that
marriage should be for love and
bring happiness – not just for
class status and money.

Evaluation

For all criteria, note whether your effort was (1) weak, (2) adequate, or (3) good to great. Answer only those that are applicable.

Met time restriction	1	2	3
Located heartbeat words	1	2	3

Strength of Examples

One or more predetermined topics matched the theme	1	2	3
Comfortable using personal example	1	2	3
Comfortable creating fictional example	1	2	3

Thesis Statement

Used heartbeat words	1	2	3
Argument based on best examples	1	2	3
Overall strength of exercise	1	2	3

Planning Session Two

Prompt:

Owing to American mobility—people moving about the country for work, a more pleasing environment, retirement, and much else—the category of long-distance friend has become a larger one than perhaps at any previous time. Some friends are not merely out of town, but out of the country. The main distinction between long-distance and other friends is that the element of regularity plays a much smaller part in out-of-town friendships. Good feelings can certainly stay alive with out-of-town friends, but friendship doesn't get much of a workout at such distances.

—Adapted from *Friendship: An Exposé*, by JOSEPH EPSTEIN (Houghton Mifflin, 2006)

Assignment:

Are long-distance friendships as valuable as those formed with people we have regular face-to-face contact with? Organize and compose an essay that establishes your viewpoint on this issue. Substantiate it with examples and evidence derived from what you have read, studied, experienced, or observed.

Heartbeat word(s) "long-distance" "friendships" "contact" "valuable"

Match theme to content (In what topics does the theme of friendship appear? Is the idea of long-distance friendships in any of these topics?)

Aeneid - best friend with Achates

Hamlet → Horatio and Hamlet v. Rosencrantz + Guildenstern.

P+P → Charlotte, neighbor. Bingley knows completely of relationship.

James — long-distance friendship better than everyday friendship.

TKMB → Dill is long distance but lives 4 Finch summer.

Thesis statement

~~A long-distance friendship is just as valuable as one formed between people in constant contact.~~

A friendship is most valuable between people who are in regular contact with each other.

Best examples

Pride + Prejudice → Bingley
leaves the countryside so his
relationship with the Bennet family
completely ends.

Evaluation

For each criteria, note whether your effort was (1) weak, (2) adequate, or (3) good to great. Answer only those that are applicable.

Met time restriction	1	2	3
Located heartbeat words	1	2	3

Strength of Examples

One or more predetermined topics matched the theme	1	2	3
Comfortable using personal example	1	2	3
Comfortable creating fictional example	1	2	3

Thesis Statement

Used heartbeat words	1	2	3
Argument based on best examples	1	2	3
Overall strength of exercise	1	2	3

Planning Session Three

Prompt:

Mankind likes to think in terms of extreme opposites. It is given to formulating its beliefs in terms of Either-Ors, between which it recognizes no intermediate possibilities. When forced to recognize that the extremes cannot be acted upon, it is still inclined to hold that they are all right in theory but that when it comes to practical matters circumstances compel us to compromise.

—Adapted from *Experience and Education*,
by JOHN DEWEY (Kappa Delta Pi, 1938)

Assignment:

Should we base our beliefs on Either-Ors, or does the truth lie between extremes? Organize and compose an essay that establishes your viewpoint on this issue. Substantiate it with examples and evidence derived from what you have read, studied, experienced, or observed.

Heartbeat word(s) _____

Match theme to content (In what topics does the theme of extremes appear? Is the idea of basing beliefs on extremes in any of these topics?)

_____

_____

_____

_____

_____

_____

Thesis statement

The truth can be found only at the extremes.

As seen in both my experience and the life of Prince Hamlet, the truth lies only at either extreme.

Best examples

Hamlet

Ride -a-long (me).

Evaluation

For each criteria, note whether your effort was (1) weak, (2) adequate, or (3) good to great. Answer only those that are applicable.

Met time restriction	1	(2)	3
Located heartbeat words	1	(2)	3

Strength of Examples

One or more predetermined topics matched the theme	1	2	(3)
Comfortable using personal example	1	2	3
Comfortable creating fictional example	(1)	2	3

Thesis Statement

Used heartbeat words	1	(2)	3
Argument based on best examples	1	(2)	3
Overall strength of exercise	1	(2)	3

Planning Session Four

Prompt:

At this point in human history we have enough material resources to feed, clothe, shelter, and educate every living individual on Earth. That such resources exist is not merely a utopian fantasy, it is a reality about which there is little serious debate. Nonetheless, a quick look around most any part of the globe tells us just how far we are from achieving any of these goals. Most of the world's population is now growing up in winner-take-all economies, where the main goal of individuals is to get whatever they can for themselves: to each according to his greed.

—Adapted from *The High Price of Materialism*,
by TIM KASSER (MIT Press, 2003)

Assignment:

Is humankind more materialistic than ever before? Organize and compose an essay that establishes your viewpoint on this issue. Substantiate it with examples and evidence derived from what you have read, studied, experienced, or observed.

Heartbeat word(s) _more 'materialistic'_

Match theme to content (In what topics does the theme of materialism appear? Is the idea of materialism a growing problem in any of these topics?)

P+P → entailment marriges so important b/c of materialism — real estate + things.

Hamlet →

TKMB → Great Depression

Aeneid →

Emperor of Ice Cream → he is more important than the death of a woman because he gives ice cream — symbolizes greediness and problem of materialism

I once met a Buddhist monk who said that materialism breaks the link between man and nature.

Thesis statement

Both Wallace Stevens and a Buddhist monk would agree with me that materialism is becoming a growing problem for humanity.

Best examples

Empire of Icecream

"Buddhist monk"

Evaluation

For each criteria, note whether your effort was (1) weak, (2) adequate, or (3) good to great. Answer only those that are applicable.

Met time restriction	1	2	(3)
Located heartbeat words	1	2	3

Strength of Examples

One or more predetermined topics matched the theme	(1)	2	3
Comfortable using personal example	1	2	(3)
Comfortable creating fictional example	1	2	(3)

Thesis Statement

Used heartbeat words	1	(2)	3
Argument based on best examples	1	(2)	3
Overall strength of exercise	1	2	(3)

Planning Session Five

Prompt:

Optimism is power. This is a secret discovered by all who succeed against great odds. Nelson Mandela, Ernest Shackleton, Eleanor Roosevelt—all admitted that what got them through tough times was an ability to focus on the positive. They understood what Claude Bristol called "the magic of believing." Optimistic people tend to succeed not simply because they believe that everything will turn out right, but because the expectation of success makes them work harder.

—Adapted from *50 Success Classics*,
by Tom Butler-Bowdon (Nicholas Brealey, 2004)

Assignment:

Is optimism a key ingredient of success? Organize and compose an essay that establishes your viewpoint on this issue. Substantiate it with examples and evidence derived from what you have read, studied, experienced, or observed.

Heartbeat word(s) ___"optimism" "success"___

Match theme to content (In what topics does the theme of optimism appear? Is the idea of optimism linked to success in any of these topics?)

Hamlet →

Aeneid → and perhaps someday
we will enjoy remembering these things.
(Trojan War).

P+P → Darcy feels that the elopement
of Lydia and Wickham will turn out
better than the Bernet family imagines.

TKMB → starts of with the quote "nothing to fear
but fear itself"

B) Break computer → it is possible?!

Thesis statement

In for the United *FDR* to be successful in getting *America* through the Great Depression, and for Aeneas to be successful in founding Rome, they had to ~~en~~ be optimistic.

Best examples

FDR quote

Aeneid.

Evaluation

For each criteria, note whether your effort was (1) weak, (2) adequate, or (3) good to great. Answer only those that are applicable.

Met time restriction	1	(2)	3
Located heartbeat words	1	2	(3)

Strength of Examples

One or more predetermined topics matched the theme	1	2	3
Comfortable using personal example	1	2	3
Comfortable creating fictional example	1	2	3

Thesis Statement

Used heartbeat words	1	2	3
Argument based on best examples	1	2	3
Overall strength of exercise	1	2	3

What's Next?

Review the evaluations for each exercise. Did you see improvement, or was your first session as strong (or as weak) as your last? Here are the steps you need to take to continue building your essay planning skills.

If you couldn't get all three steps completed in five or six minutes: Was there one step that held you up more than the others or was it the entire exercise? Reread Chapter 3, and then find online prompts (listed in the Appendix). Complete at least five more planning sessions, concentrating only on the step(s) that took longest to complete.

If you had trouble locating the heartbeat words: Check the list of assignments on page 39 at the end of Chapter 3. Circle the heartbeat words for at least ten of them. If you selected four or more for any assignment, decide which word is not as essential to the theme as the others.

If you were unable to match at least one of your topics to the theme: First, check the theme. You probably noticed that contemporary life assignments are more difficult to match with older topics from literature and history. These are often better addressed with personal examples (here's where using fictitious examples comes in handy).

Or you may have found that one or more of your topics could have worked if you knew a little more about it. For example, the Great Depression content became much more flexible when the idea of protectionism was included. Knowing about the Smoot-Hawley Act and its results made that topic work with many more assignments. Digging a little deeper will make for richer content.

If you weren't comfortable using a personal or fictitious example: These need practice too! You probably spent an hour or more developing your academic content. While you don't need to research or review your life experiences, you may want to practice with another five assignments. Think of one personal example and one fictitious one for each (the fictitious example can be about you or a friend or relative).

If your thesis statement didn't use the heartbeat words you circled: Again, practice on five more assignments with this goal in mind. Using heartbeat words helps you create a plan that you can use quickly and consistently.

If your thesis statement wasn't based on your best examples: You probably read the assignment and chose a point of view before working through steps one and two. While that's not a bad way to come up with a thesis statement quickly, it's not effective as an overall strategy. Remember that writing this sentence last, after you've decided on the examples you want to use in your essay, will give you a plan that's grounded in your best ideas.

5 PUTTING IT ALL TOGETHER

You learned in Chapter 2 that you can develop content for your essay well before your test date. Practicing with that content, you'll become comfortable choosing and adapting your topics to fit various essay assignments. For some essays, just one of your topics may work, and you'll be able to use different themes to round out your essay. For others, three may be suitable. And for others still, you may need to discuss a friend or relative whose experiences (real or fictional) serve as perfect examples to back up your point of view.

With your topics established and your skill at responding quickly to assignments strengthened, you can begin creating complete essays. In this chapter, we'll use sample prompts and assignments to show how the content introduced in Chapter 2 can be used to write them. Every part of the essay, from body paragraphs to the quote you use in your conclusion, serves a distinct function. Here, you'll learn how to maximize the effectiveness of each part of your essay.

In Every Paragraph

In Chapter 3, you learned about prompts and assignments and how to take a stand quickly.

You discovered why it's important to determine heartbeat words to create a list of possible topics and why you should repeat them throughout your essay. This will indicate clearly to your readers that you are responding to the topic without veering off track. When a word is used in every paragraph, echoing like a heartbeat, it will serve as a reminder that you are responding to the assignment. To emphasize how effective and important they are, you'll see more examples of heartbeat words in the body paragraph section of this chapter.

The Introduction

After four to six minutes of planning, you'll begin writing with an introductory paragraph. Include the following in this paragraph:

- **your thesis statement,** in which you take a stand on the issue presented in the prompt, fully addressing the assignment and using the heartbeat word(s): *While postponing choices can lead to negative consequences, those consequences are typically not dangerous.*
- **three points to back up your stand** (three predetermined topics, or two plus a personal or fictional one)

Let's look again at the first example from Chapter 3. The assignment was: *Can it be dangerous to postpone choices?* In four steps, we (1) brainstormed with the content developed in Chapter 2, (2) identified three strong examples of the danger of postponing choices (see pages 35–36), (3) answered "yes" to the assignment question, and (4) wrote a thesis statement that both answered the question and used the heartbeat words *dangerous* and *choices*: *Postponing choices can not only lead to negative consequences, but those consequences can be dangerous.*

Begin with your thesis statement. Then follow it with two or three sentences that generally introduce your topics:

> *Postponing choices can not only lead to negative consequences, but those consequences can be dangerous. Throughout American history and literature, there are many examples that illustrate this fact. Set in the Colonial period, Nathanial Hawthorne's* The Scarlet Letter *introduces the character of Dimmesdale, the minister who chooses, with deadly consequences, to keep a secret. In the early twentieth century, as the United States and much of the world found itself in the worst economic depression on record, the country delayed*

for two years a decision that would eventually lead to economic recovery. And in modern times, our slow response to climate change means we are continuing to damage our planet.

THE POWER OF INDENTATIONS

Remember reading about essay length rumors in Chapter 1? We can't confirm that shorter essays with few paragraphs are given lower scores by the computer that scans them, but we can recognize that longer essays that are clearly divided into at least four paragraphs score higher. Don't make the computer, or your scorer, wonder where one paragraph ends and another begins. By exaggerating your indentations, you're highlighting the structure of your essay (and taking up some space that you'd otherwise have to fill with words).

Notice that in this paragraph the author has found an organizing principle for his three examples. Not only are they all American, but they represent three time periods. He sets each example in chronological order. Here are some additional points to consider:

- **Tone:** Essay starts with a confidently worded thesis statement, then refers to it as "fact" in the second sentence.
- **Heartbeat words:** Both words appear in the thesis statement, and the word *chooses* is also in the third sentence. Synonyms include *delayed* and *decision*.
- **Three examples:** All are very briefly introduced without giving too much away.

Here's another example of an introduction using the same material:

Postponing choices can not only lead to negative consequences, but those consequences can be dangerous. This is not always the case, but there are plenty of examples of where it is. In The Scarlet Letter, *Dimmesdale decides he shouldn't tell anyone he is Pearl's father. During the Great Depression, the United States took a long time before dropping the gold standard. Today, we are not doing enough to combat climate change, even though many countries are making a big effort to do so.*

How do these two introductions compare? In the second introduction did you notice the following?

- **Tone:** Essay begins confidently, but the second sentence admits that *this is not always the case.*
- **Heartbeat words:** They are used in thesis statement only.
- **Three examples:** Too many details are used, and it is not clear how they tie in with the thesis.

Stronger Introductions: the Hook

There are good introductions, and then there are great introductions. Because this first paragraph makes such as strong impression on your reader, taking your essay from a solid 5 to a 6 can be as simple as creating an introductory hook. A hook grabs your reader from the first sentence. It's meant to be startling, different, and memorable. While starting with your thesis statement can be a solid opening, consider how much more powerful the second example below is:

> *Postponing choices can not only lead to negative consequences, but those consequences can be dangerous.*
>
> *By ending* The Scarlet Letter *with Arthur Dimmesdale's dramatic death, Nathaniel Hawthorne teaches us that his character's delay in making an important choice took not just a mental toll, but a physical one as well.*

Using the second example and tying it directly to your thesis statement is more compelling than just starting with the thesis statement. To use this technique, you'll need to tell a very quick story with that first sentence, and then follow it with your thesis statement (modified if necessary). Note below how the introduction works as a whole:

> *By ending* The Scarlet Letter *with Arthur Dimmesdale's dramatic death, Nathaniel Hawthorne teaches us that his character's delay in making an important choice took not just a mental toll, but a physical one as well. Postponing choices, in Hawthorne's novel as well as in our history, can not only lead to negative consequences, but those consequences can be dangerous. In the early twentieth century, as the United States and much of the world found itself in the worst economic depression on record, the country delayed for two years a decision that would eventually lead to economic recovery. And in modern times, our slow response to climate change means we are continuing to damage our planet.*

Here are two other hook options:

1. **Ask a question.** Reword the assignment question: *Can simply postponing a choice create negative, or even dangerous consequences? Lessons in American literature and history tell us it can.*

2. **Use a statistic.** *The Earth's surface temperature is predicted to rise another one degree during the twenty-first century, bringing it to its highest level in over 1,000 years.* A note on statistics: Your readers are English and/or writing teachers, not scientists or historians. Unless you're using numbers that are common knowledge, they probably won't be familiar with them.

Exercise

Does having a plan for your future help keep the concerns of daily living in better perspective?

Using the examples and thesis statement you developed on page 39 in Chapter 3, write an introductory paragraph. Try one of the hook techniques in your first sentence.

_____

_____

_____

_____

_____

_____

_____

Body Paragraphs

Each of your three body paragraphs has the same purpose: to support your thesis statement. They achieve that purpose, and your essay gets a higher score, when they also do the following:

- guide the reader with transition words
- show your command of written English, including grammar and vocabulary
- make each at least four sentences long, to bring your essay to one and a half to two pages total
- repeat the heartbeat words to remind the reader you are staying on topic
- use examples and evidence to back up your points
- use at least two types of sentence structures

Transition Words

You use transition words all the time. They help make your ideas clear and orderly, emphasizing, comparing, contrasting, locating in time and space, beginning, and concluding. They're listed here not because you need to learn them, but because you need to be aware of them as you write your SAT Essay.

Transition words literally guide your reader. They make it clear that you are moving from one point to another, that you're drawing a conclusion, and that you see how each piece of evidence fits in the context of your argument. They also make the point that you have planned your writing and are following that plan.

Transition words can be used to build that level of confidence that is so important in a persuasive essay. Move from your thesis statement to a sentence beginning with *It follows that*, and it will be clear to your reader that there is a strong and logical connection. The word *nevertheless* demonstrates that while there may be another way of thinking about one of your examples, your way is correct.

Transition words are especially important as you move from one body paragraph to another. Starting body paragraph two, for example, with *Similarly* means the point you are about to make reinforces and adds to the one in the previous paragraph.

The following are common transition words and their uses:

Showing location: *above, along, amid, among, between, by, following, near, off, over, throughout*

Showing time: *after, afterwards, finally, first, later, meanwhile, next, now, second, simultaneously, soon, subsequently, then, third, until, while*

Comparing: *also, as, like, likewise, in the same way, similarly, while*

Contrasting: *although, but, conversely, despite, even though, however, nevertheless, on the contrary, though, yet*

Emphasizing: *again, especially, for this reason, in fact, to repeat*

Concluding: *as a result, because, finally, in conclusion, last, therefore*

Adding information: *additionally, along with, also, and, another, as well, besides, for example, for instance, in addition, moreover*

WHICH EXAMPLE SHOULD YOU USE FIRST?

Essays you write for your classes should typically start with your weakest example. It's more interesting to build up to the best, most important points. But with just 25 minutes to write your SAT essay, it makes more sense to start with your best example. If you do run out of time (and by using this book, your chances of doing that have lessened considerably), you'll be working on the least interesting example rather than the most.

Grammar and Vocabulary

The writer's workshop lessons in Chapters 6 and 7 are designed to refresh your knowledge of the major issues involving grammar, mechanics, and word choice. But what about those SAT words? Expanding your vocabulary before taking the test has always been a great idea: Using college-level words will impress your readers (part of your score is based on evidence of a varied and intelligent vocabulary), and many of the Critical Reading multiple-choice questions, including those involving passage-based reading, test vocabulary. But which words do you need to know?

Every SAT prep book and hundreds of websites have lists of SAT words. Some are a few hundred words while others list thousands. There is no way to predict which words the College Board will use on a particular test, and it's also unreasonable to expect that you'll learn thousands of new words between now and your test date(s). In the Appendix of this book, there is a list of 50 words that appear frequently on the SAT and definitely qualify as intelligent.

In addition to memorizing them, it's possible to plan ahead to use a few of them in your essay. Refer to the background sentences you wrote for your content topics in Chapter 2. Those are the sentences you'll be able to plug into almost any essay to set the scene for your topic. Check them for a word or words you can replace with more dynamic ones. Here are some examples:

Before inclusion of SAT words:

American inventor Thomas Edison (1847–1931) has been described as more responsible than anyone else for creating the modern world. In his research laboratory in Menlo Park, New Jersey, he invented the phonograph, made the electric lightbulb, and started the motion picture industry.

After:

American inventor Thomas Edison (1847–1931) has been <u>characterized</u> as more responsible than anyone else for creating the modern world. In his research laboratory in Menlo Park, New Jersey, he invented the phonograph, <u>devised</u> the electric lightbulb, and <u>pioneered</u> the motion picture industry.

Before inclusion of SAT words:

On October 29, 1929, the United States stock market crashed. This event, along with bank failures, consumers' fears that kept them from making purchases, bad governmental policies, and even the environment came together to create a worldwide economic collapse. Recovery would take nearly a decade.

After:

On October 29, 1929, the United States stock market crashed. This event, coupled with bank failures, consumers' <u>trepidation</u> that kept them from making purchases, <u>protectionist</u> governmental policies, and even the environment <u>conspired</u> to create a worldwide economic collapse. Recovery would take nearly a decade.

Exercise

Check the background sentences you wrote in Chapter 2 on pages 21–26. Rewrite each below, substituting SAT words where appropriate (aim for at least two words per topic).

Topic 1 _During the reign of emperor Augustus, Vergil wrote the Aeneid. This epic poem is the story of the founding of Rome beginning with the Trojan War. (account, partly mythical, partly historical ...)_

Topic 2 _William Shakespeare's Hamlet tells the story of a prince whose daughter is his obsession. Hamlet's father murdered by his own brother, and must be avenged by his son._

Topic 3 _Written by Jane Austen in 1813, Pride and Prejudice ... account of marry is for love. Our heroine Elizabeth_

fights for his cause, while our hero
Darcy does not marry someone with
his social class.

Topic 4 Harper Lee's To kill
a Mockingbird is the story of a
young girl named scout growing up
during the Great Depression. It is
also a story of prejudice and
racism.

Topic 5

Topic 6

_____

_____

Length and Structure

Body paragraphs have four unique sections. As you write, be conscious of including each, and you will not only be able to quickly tie your example to your thesis, but also get the length that you're aiming for.

Part One: Answers the question, *Why does this example support your thesis statement?*

Part Two: Includes prepared background on your example.

Part Three: Answers the question, *How does this example* specifically *support your thesis statement?*

Part Four: Concludes by addressing the question from Part One.

Here's an example:

> *Perspective is an emotional viewpoint; it is an individual's belief about what is going on around him. One strong component of perspective, especially during troubled times, is hope. When you have hope, your plan for the future includes improvement of the current situation, and that belief makes it possible to go on. Pablo Picasso's mural* Guernica, *which he painted for the 1937 World's Fair in Paris, depicts hope amid the horrors of war. In the hands of a dying soldier is a flower in full bloom. At the top of the mural is a lightbulb surrounded by rays like the sun. The flower and the lightbulb help to keep the violence and tragedy of armed conflict in perspective. They point to the future with hope, and therefore help lessen the pain of the present.*

Did you notice the following?

- Three sentences were needed to make the connection between the example and the thesis.
- The background sentences (see page 36 in Chapter 3) were modified.
- Heartbeat words *planning* and *perspective* were used four times.
- Specific details (the flower and the lightbulb) were used.
- Transition words (*amid, especially, therefore*) help guide the reader.
- Sentence structure is varied: Some are short and simple while others are made up of a few phrases and clauses.

Examples and Evidence

Your SAT Essay score will be based in part on how well you use appropriate examples and evidence to support your position. It's not enough to agree that planning for the future helps you keep your daily life in perspective. You must say more precisely how and/or why.

Here's what the previous example paragraph would look like without examples:

> *Perspective is an emotional viewpoint; it is an individual's belief about what is going on around him. One strong component of perspective, especially during troubled times, is hope. When you have hope. your plan for the future includes improvement from the current situation, and that belief makes it possible to go on. Pablo Picasso's mural* Guernica, *which he painted for the 1937 World's Fair in Paris, depicts hope. When you have hope, you can keep the problems of daily life in perspective.*

The reader is left wondering why the writer chose *Guernica* as an example. What about the painting specifically shows hope? It's a great start, but using the details of the flower and lightbulb take the author's point of view from questionable to authoritative.

SHOW VERSUS TELL

It's relatively easy to tell a story: *Picasso's* Guernica *is known as one of the most powerful pieces of antiwar art.* But it's more interesting to show: *With its stark, black and white images of the violence and brutality of combat—a radical departure from the glorified and heroic images of the past—Picasso's* Guernica *is known as one of the most powerful pieces of antiwar art.* It's the *details* and *evidence* in the second sentence that take it from merely telling the readers something to showing them in detail.

As you practice, ask whether you're merely telling a story or if you're developing strong examples and showing with detail and evidence why they support your thesis.

Here's another example:

> *One way to keep the events of daily life in perspective is to work on current problems to lessen their impact on the future. In other words, planning to have a better future can help us deal with the issues we face today. For example, the news about climate change isn't good. The Earth has become about one degree (Fahrenheit) warmer in the last century, and every day we hear more bad news about the effects of global warming. But people are doing something about these effects. Knowing that efforts like these are being made helps to put the negative news in perspective.*

This paragraph does a few things well: It has a strong link to the assignment, sentence structure is varied, an appropriate background sentence and heartbeat words are used, and the length is appropriate. But the examples and evidence are missing. Here the problem is corrected:

> *One way to keep the events of daily life in perspective is to work on current problems to lessen their impact on the future. In other words, planning to have a better future can help us deal with the issues we face today. For example, the news about climate change isn't good. The Earth has become about one degree (Fahrenheit) warmer in the last century, and every day we hear about how the polar ice caps are melting and that warmer ocean temperatures are causing stronger and more frequent hurricanes. But people are doing something about these effects. Their efforts include reducing greenhouse gas emissions and searching for cleaner forms of energy. Some scientists are even working on geo-engineering, which would allow us to manipulate the Earth's climate. Politicians are debating what needs to be done, and many, including the 186 leaders who signed on to the Kyoto Protocol, are committing financial resources to researching solutions. Knowing that efforts like these are being made helps to put the negative news in perspective.*

Sentence Structure

One of the last things you'll probably be thinking about on testing day is varying your sentence structure. But it's important. Of the five areas on which your score is based, one is varied sentence structure, so you can be sure readers are looking for it.

Note the difference between the following two examples:

President Richard Nixon was elected in November of 1968. He defeated George McGovern four years later. McGovern was against the Vietnam War. The 1972 election was a landslide.

President Richard Nixon was elected in November of 1968. Four years later, he was reelected in a landslide, defeating the anti-Vietnam War candidate George McGovern.

Instead of four short sentences that follow a noun-verb pattern, the second example has one short sentence and one long one that includes clauses (*four years later* and *in a landslide*) to break the pattern. A section in Chapter 7, Punctuation of Complex Sentences (page 96), explains how to use punctuation to vary sentence structure. Pay careful attention and consciously and correctly use semicolons, colons, parentheses, and dashes to create more complex sentences (colons and dashes add a tone of authority that can help assert your point of view more strongly).

Exercise

After reviewing the section on Punctuation of Complex Sentences, go to the background information you wrote in Chapter 2. Rewrite it, including at least one simple and one complex sentence. By practicing how to do this now, you're much more likely to include a variety of sentence structures in your finished essay.

Topic 1 ___The Aeneid is an epic poem___

___about the founding of Rome.___

___Vergil the prophet about how the___

___Roman came from defeat in the___

___Trojan war to success in the___

___Augustan Golden Age to began.___

Topic 2 _In the Shakespearean tragedy, Hamlet, the hero must decide whether or not he should avenge his murdered father by murdering his king._

Topic 3 _Despite her parents' discouragement of a marriage concept merely for love, Ms. Darcy is determined to marry Elizabeth despite their differences because he truly loves her._

Topic 4 _Harper Lee's A Mockingbird is a heartwarming novel about Scout growing up in Alabama during the Great Depression. It is also a powerful tale about prejudice. Absorbing_

Topic 5 _____

_____

_____

_____

_____

_____

Topic 6 _____

_____

_____

_____

_____

_____

The Conclusion

Leaving your reader with a strong impression just seconds before he or she assigns a score to your essay is a great strategy. But with just a couple of minutes left, how can you do more than simply summarize your writing?

First, keep your expectations reasonable. Aim for two or three sentences, and make the first a rewording of your thesis statement. It might sound redundant, but it serves an important purpose: By including a reiterated thesis, you remind the reader that you had a strong idea and followed it through to the end of your essay. What can you follow it with? Here are three ideas for quick yet memorable endings:

1. Offer a solution or suggestion:

> *Keeping our daily lives in perspective can be as simple as planning for the future. If we take steps now to improve our situation later, such as by imposing banking regulations that will help us avoid future recessions, our day-to-day problems will be easier to handle.*

Did you notice the following?
- The reworked thesis repeats the heartbeat words.
- The second sentence begins with *If.*
- The solution or suggestion is specific (uses *such as* followed by an example).

2. Include a quote. You came up with some quotes in Chapter 2. Now is your chance to use one if it works in the context of your essay:

> *By learning from our past and creating plans for the future based on what we learn, we can keep today's problems in perspective. The refrain from the Great Depression, "Brother, can you spare a dime?" echoes true again today. But just as the economy recovered after the Depression, we can be confident that today's situation will also improve.*

> *Success often depends on effort. Thomas Edison once said, "Genius is 1% inspiration and 99% perspiration." Edison would have agreed that nothing takes the place of hard work. As good as his ideas were, it was the time he spent trying, failing, and retrying that was the key to his success.*

3. Create an analogy. Describe a situation that illustrates your thesis, introducing it with *Just as* and concluding it with *so too can*:

> *By learning from our past and creating plans for the future based on what we learn, we can keep today's problems in perspective. Just as an athlete keeps her "eye on the prize" to get through grueling workouts, so too can we focus on the big picture to take steps toward our future.*

Exercise

Complete three conclusions using this as your first sentence: *Keeping our daily lives in perspective can be as simple as planning for the future.*

1. Offer a solution or suggestion. _____

_____

_____

_____

_____

_____

2. Use a quote from the content you developed in Chapter 2 or another of your choosing.

_____

_____

_____

_____

3. Create an analogy _____

_____

_____

_____

_____

_____

6

WRITER'S WORKSHOP PART I: WORD CHOICE

Words have power. Used well, they convey your ideas accurately and precisely. Used poorly, they can confuse, misinform, and even make your reader think you're not as smart as you really are. In this chapter, we'll examine the syntax (word choice) issues you need to understand to write a great essay.

Be Precise

"A well chosen word has often sufficed to stop a flying army, to change defeat into victory, and to save an empire."

—EMILE DE GIRARDIN

The words you use must deliver the maximum impact. Choosing appropriate, specific adjectives and adverbs (modifiers) makes your point clear, and you can convey ideas with better style and more shades of meaning. Consider the difference between these two sentences:

Tom puts his hat on and walks away.

Tom Wessels slaps his felt hat over his bushy hair and starts striding away with the confident gait of a hiker.

The latter example allows you to hear the voice and impressions of the writer, giving a more accurate and interesting picture of the action. The first sentence is simply dull. Using modifiers allows your reader to more closely connect to your text and gives your writing a visual and emotional power that is more memorable.

Examples of Powerful, Precise Adjectives and Adverbs
- *directly* involved
- *unflagging* dedication
- *promptly* accepted
- *productive* discussion
- *grueling* game
- *instinctively* aware
- *influential* teacher
- *invaluable* learning experience

Be Accurate

Pay attention to the meaning of every word you use. There are many English words that look and/or sound similar but have very different meanings. If you are unsure of a definition, look it up. One wrong word—using *illicit* when you mean *elicit*, for example—can completely change the meaning of an otherwise well-written sentence. A number of these errors can also make your reader question your grasp of the language.

The following is a list of the most commonly confused word pairs or groups, with brief definitions. Check your essay for them, making sure you have used the correct word. You might want to make flash cards for each pair or group and use the cards to learn the definitions so your future writing improves as well.

COMMONLY CONFUSED WORDS

Word	Quick Definition
accept	recognize
except	excluding
access	means of approaching
excess	extra
affect:	to influence
effect (noun)	result
effect (verb)	to bring about
assure	to certify, convince
ensure	to make certain, guarantee
insure	to insure, back up financially
beside	next to
besides	in addition to
bibliography	list of writings
biography	a life story
complement	match
compliment	praise
decent	well-mannered
descent	decline, fall
desert	arid, sandy region
dessert	sweet served after a meal
disburse	to pay
disperse	to spread out
disinterested	no strong opinion either way
uninterested	not concerned
elicit	to stir up
illicit	illegal
farther	beyond (distance)
further	additional (amount)

Word	Quick Definition
imply	hint, suggest
infer	assume, deduce
personal	pertaining to the individual
personnel	employees
principal (adjective)	main
principal (noun)	person in charge
principle	standard
than	in contrast to
then	next
their	belonging to them
there	in a place
they're	they are
who	substitute for he, she, or they
whom	substitute for him, her, or them
your	belonging to you
you're	you are

Choosing the right words also means being aware of the many commonly misused ones. You may find examples of misused words in the media, on billboards and other signs, in speech, and in everyday writing. Even when used incorrectly, many these words can look acceptable to some writers. But they will stand out as glaring errors to admissions officers. Take the time to learn them, and avoid embarrassing mistakes.

SAT TIP

Many of these misused words appear in Writing and Critical Reading multiple-choice questions. Learn them now and keep an eye out for them later.

COMMONLY MISUSED WORDS

Word	Meaning
among	a comparison or reference to three or more people or things
between	a comparison or reference to two people or things
amount	when you cannot count the items to which you are referring, and when referring to singular nouns
number	when you can count the items to which you are referring, and when referring to plural nouns
anxious	nervous
eager	enthusiastic or looking forward to something
bring	moving something toward the speaker
take	moving something away from the speaker
can	used to state ability
may	used to state permission
each other	when referring to two people or things
one another	when referring to three or more people or things
e.g.	an abbreviation for the Latin *exempli gratia*, meaning *free example* or *for example*
i.e.	an abbreviation for the Latin *id est*, meaning *it is* or *that is*
feel bad	used when talking about emotional feelings
feel badly	used when talking about physical feelings
fewer	when you can count the items
less	when you cannot count the items
good	an adjective, which describes a person, place, or thing
well	an adverb, which describes an action or verb
its	belonging to it

Word	Meaning
it's	contraction of *it is*
lay	the action of placing or putting an item somewhere; a transitive verb, meaning something you do *to* something else
lie	to recline or be placed; an intransitive verb, meaning it does not act on anything or anyone else
more	used to compare one thing to one other thing
most:	used to compare one thing to more than one other thing
that	a pronoun that introduces a restrictive (or essential) clause
which	a pronoun that introduces a nonrestrictive (or unessential) clause

Stay Active

"You have such strong words at command, that they make the smallest argument seem formidable."

—GEORGE ELIOT

When a verb is active, the subject of the sentence *performs* an action. In a passive construction, the subject *receives* the action.

Active: *The bird ate the birdseed.*
Passive: *The birdseed was eaten by the bird.*

In the first sentence, the bird (the subject) performs the action, *ate*. In the second sentence, does the subject *birdseed* do anything? No; instead, it is acted upon.

Note how many more words it takes to communicate the same idea in the passive voice. This is one reason the active voice is preferred (and this also applies to your application essay). It is more direct and concise.

Instead of: *The bank account was closed by Sheila.*
Write: *Sheila closed the bank account.*

Instead of: *The active voice should be used by essay writers.*
Write: *Essay writers should use the active voice.*

That said, there are some instances when you should use the passive voice. Choose it in the following three situations:

1. You want to deliberately emphasize the receiver of the action instead of the performer: *My fender was dented three times in that parking lot.*

2. The performer is unknown: *Mani's wallet was mysteriously returned.*

3. You want to avoid mentioning the performer of the action: *The experiment resulted in a new theory.*

Eliminate Ambiguity

"Speak clearly, if you speak at all; carve every word before you let it fall."

—OLIVER WENDELL HOLMES

Using ambiguous words (that is, words with two or more possible meanings), and using the right words in the wrong order, can cause confusion. The meaning understood by the reader may not be the one intended by the writer. There are two important guidelines to follow in order to avoid ambiguity:

1. Refrain from using words and phrases with more than one meaning.

2. Be sure the words you use are in the right order to convey your intended meaning.

For example: *During my photojournalism class, I shot the model.*

This sentence can be read two ways: You shot pictures with a camera, or you shot the model with a gun. This kind of confusion can happen whenever a word has more than one possible meaning. *During my photojournalism class, I took pictures of the model* is a better sentence.

Example: *My customer ate the sandwich with the blue hat.*

Here, the *word order* of the sentence, not an individual word, causes the confusion. Did the customer eat her sandwich with her hat? Because the phrase *with the blue hat* is in the wrong place, the meaning of the sentence is unclear. Try instead: *My customer with the blue hat ate the sandwich.*

Correcting Ambiguous Language

Ambiguous: *When reaching for the phone, the coffee spilled on the table.*
Clear: *The coffee spilled on the table when you reached for the phone.*

Ambiguous: *I went to see the doctor with a severe headache.*
Clear: *I went to see the doctor because I had a severe headache.*

Ambiguous: *The famous artist drew stares when he entered the room.*
Clear: *The famous artist received stares when he entered the room.*

Ambiguous: *When writing on the computer, the spell-checker often comes in handy.*
Clear: *The spell-checker often comes in handy when I am writing on the computer.*

7
WRITER'S WORKSHOP PART TWO: GRAMMAR AND MECHANICS

A grammatical error or misspelled word won't be held against you. But an essay that continuously breaks the conventions of the language will get a lower score. Many of the issues presented in this chapter are tested in the SAT multiple-choice Writing section, and understanding them will improve your essay writing as well. Take the time to review these grammar and mechanics elements, which typically form the greatest number of errors on the SAT Essay. Learn them now and you'll score higher on the test!

Subject/Verb Agreement

Agreement refers to number: If you have a singular subject, you need a singular verb. Plural subjects take plural verbs. To achieve subject/verb agreement, first determine whether your subject is singular or plural, and then pair it with the correct verb form.

These examples use the verb *to be*, which is irregular. (I *am*, you *are*, he/she/it *is*, they *are*, I *was*, you *were*, he/she/it *was*, they *were*)

> **Instead of:** *Tim and Fran is a great couple.*
> **Write:** *Tim and Fran are a great couple.* (*Tim and Fran* is a plural subject that takes a plural verb.)

Instead of: *One of my friends are going to your school.*
Write: *One of my friends is going to school.* (*One* is a singular subject that takes singular verb.)

When It Gets Tricky

Agreement can be difficult to determine when sentences are complex (that is, when they don't follow a subject followed by verb pattern like the examples above) or when the subject is a compound (made up of more than one noun). Common examples include sentences in which the subject follows the verb, as well as those beginning with *there is/are* and *here is/are*. When editing your work, remember to first figure out whether your subject is singular or plural, and then match it to the correct verb.

Instead of: *There is too many meetings scheduled on Tuesday morning.*
Write: *There are too many meetings scheduled on Tuesday morning.*

Instead of: *Here are the report you asked me to write.*
Write: *Here is the report you asked me to write.*

When compound subjects are connected by *and* (pencils *and* pens; the ball, the bat, *and* the mitt), they are plural. When they're connected by *or* (World War I *or* World War II; biology, chemistry, *or* physics), they are singular. Confusion can set in when the nouns forming the compound subject are both singular and plural and connected by *or*. Here are two examples:

Lee or his friends are driving too fast.

Was it his friends or Lee who was driving too fast?

Both sentences are correct because when you have a compound subject made up of at least one singular subject and one plural subject connected by *or*, the verb must agree with the subject that is *closest* to it. In the first case, *friends* is plural, so the plural verb *are* is correct. In the second, *Lee* is singular, so the singular *was* is correct.

Run-On Sentences and Fragments

These are two of the most common errors on SAT essays. They are formed by incorrectly joining two or more independent clauses (complete sentences that should stand on their own) or by leaving out either the subject or verb from a sentence.

Run-Ons

I was on the soccer team, I enjoy playing golf.

This sentence contains two independent clauses (*I was on the soccer team*, and *I enjoy playing golf*). Because they can stand alone, they can't be joined with a comma. Run-on sentences can be corrected by breaking them into two or more complete sentences, by adding a conjunction (a connecting word such as *and*, *but*, *yet*, or *so*), or by changing the punctuation. Here's a correct version followed by another example:

I was on the soccer team, and I also enjoy playing golf.

When spring break is over, we will get back to work, there will be plenty of studying to do before finals.

The clause *when spring break is over* is correctly attached to *we will get back to work* with a comma. But the independent clause *there will be plenty of studying to do before finals* cannot be joined to the first part of the sentence with only a comma. It is a complete sentence that can stand alone, so if it remains part of the longer sentence, it must be connected with a period or semicolon.

Fragments

Fragments are groups of words that are presented as sentences but lack a subject, a verb, or both.

The well-dressed man. Walked to school in the rain.

In the first fragment, the verb is missing. All we have is a subject. What did the well-dressed man do? In the second fragment, the subject is missing. Who walked in the rain? To correct sentence fragments, determine what is missing (subject or verb) and add it, or change the parts of speech to convert a word into the missing part. Note that number of words has nothing to do with distinguishing fragments from sentences—fragments can be long!

> **Instead of:** *My older sister Ellen, who traveled to Japan.*
> **Write:** *My older sister Ellen traveled to Japan.*

> **Instead of:** *Taking a taxi when it is raining to keep her shoes from being ruined by the water.*
> **Write:** *Taking a taxi when it is raining keeps her shoes from being ruined by the water.*

Apostrophe and Comma Misuse

Apostrophes are used to form contractions, indicate possession or ownership, and form certain plurals. Eight rules cover all of the situations in which they may appear:

1. Add *'s* to form the singular possessive, even when the noun ends in *s*:
   - The *school's* lunchroom needs to be cleaned.
   - The *drummer's* solo received a standing ovation.
   - *Mr. Perkins's* persuasive essay was very convincing.

2. A few plurals, not ending in *s*, also form the possessive by adding *'s*:
   - The *children's* toys were found in every room of the house.
   - The line for the *women's* restroom was too long.
   - *Men's* shirts come in a variety of neck sizes.

3. Possessive plural nouns already ending in *s* need only the apostrophe added:
   - The *customers'* access codes are confidential.
   - The *students'* grades improved each semester.
   - The flight *attendants'* uniforms were blue and white.

4. Indefinite pronouns show ownership by the addition of *'s*:
   - *Everyone's* hearts were in the right place.
   - *Somebody's* dog was barking all night.
   - It was *no one's* fault that we lost the game.

5. Possessive pronouns never have apostrophes, even though some may end in *s*:
   - *Our* car is up for sale.
   - *Your* garden is beautiful.
   - *His* handwriting is difficult to read.

6. Use an *'s* to form the plurals of letters, figures, and numbers where it would be unclear without an apostrophe. It is also used with certain expressions of time and money. The expressions of time and money do not indicate ownership in the usual sense:
   - She has a hard time pronouncing *s's*.
   - My report card had three *A's*. (Without the apostrophe, this could be misread as the word *as*.)
   - The project was the result of a *year's* worth of work.

7. Show possession in the last word when using names of organizations and businesses, in hyphenated words, and in joint ownership:
   - *Sam and Janet's* graduation was three months ago.
   - I went to visit my *great-grandfather's* alma mater.
   - *The Future Farmers of America's* meeting was moved to Monday.

8. Apostrophes form contractions by taking the place of the missing letter or number:
   - *We're* going out of town next week.
   - *She's* going to write the next proposal.
   - My supervisor was in the class of *'89*.

The number one apostrophe error occurs with the simple word *it*. The addition of *'s* to the word *it* doesn't form the possessive, but rather the contraction *it's*, meaning *it is*. The possessive form of the word (meaning *belonging to it*) has no apostrophe. If you're not sure which one to use, substitute *it is*—if it works, you need the apostrophe.

Misplacing commas or leaving them out when they're called for can confuse meaning and create sloppy writing. These six rules will guide you in the correct usage of commas:

1. Use a comma to separate items in a series, including the last two items. This comma is known as the *serial comma*. One of the most famous examples

highlighting the need for this comma is a book dedication: "To my parents, Ayn Rand and God." It appears that the author's parents are Ayn Rand and God, whereas if there was a serial comma after Rand, it would be clear that the author was dedicating the book to 1) his parents, 2) Ayn Rand, and 3) God.

2. Use a comma with the conjunctions *for, and, nor, but, or,* and *yet* (remember the mnemonic FANBOY) to join two independent clauses. This comma may be dropped if the clauses are very short.
   - *He left for the Bahamas, but she went to Mexico.*
   - *I am neither excited about the idea, nor am I even thinking about using it.*

3. Use a comma to separate adjectives when the word *and* makes sense between them.
   - **Right:** *That was the most depressing, poorly directed movie I've ever seen!*
   - **Wrong:** *It was a bleak, November day.* (*November day* is the subject, modified by *bleak*—you wouldn't say *bleak and November day.*)
   - **Wrong:** *He wore a bright, red tie.* (*Bright* modifies the color red, not the tie. You wouldn't say *bright and red tie.*)

4. Use a comma after introductory phrases.
   - *Since she is leaving on vacation next Friday, she scheduled a replacement for her shift.*
   - *As the Cabinet considered the effect of the gas tax, they asked many citizens to share their opinions.*

5. Use commas to set off words and phrases that are not an integral part of the sentence.
   - *Jill, Jack's wife, works at the bank.*
   - *Henry's penchant for one-liners, while annoying to his family, delights his friends.*

6. Use commas to set off quotations, dates, and titles.
   - *Napoleon is said to have remarked, "The word* impossible *is not in my dictionary."*
   - *On July 4, 1776, the United States of America declared its independence.*
   - *Robert Zia, MD, is my general practitioner.*

Commas can create a grammatical error. When two complete sentences are joined by a comma, creating a run-on sentence, the error is called a comma splice. To correct it, you must do one of the following:
- replace the comma with a period, forming two sentences
- replace the comma with a semicolon
- join the two clauses with a conjunction such as *and*, *because*, or *so*

Accidental Shifts

Shifts are movements from one form to another. In grammar, the three most common shifts involve verb tenses, pronouns, and the active/passive voice. When these movements are made accidentally, they can cause confusion. Shifts are also one of the College Board's favorite grammatical errors—expect to see a few examples in the SAT Writing section.

Verb Tenses

Verb tenses must be consistent within each sentence and paragraph. Because they represent time (past, present, and future), shifting them can cause confusion.

If you make a mistake, your grade went down.

If you make a mistake refers to something that may happen in the future. But *grade went down* is in the past tense. We don't know if the speaker is referring to something that already happened or something that may happen. The key to avoiding verb tense shifts is to be aware of the tense you're writing in and use it consistently.

Instead of: *I had never been to London, but I will feel right at home there.*
Write: *I had never been to London, but I felt right at home there.*

Instead of: *Last year, the governor said he is campaigning for our candidate.*
Write: *Last year, the governor said he would campaign for our candidate,* or *Last year, the governor said he was campaigning for our candidate.*

Pronouns

Pronouns take the place of nouns and may be masculine or feminine, singular or plural. Shifting pronoun types within a sentence is another way to confuse your reader.

> *If they want to succeed, one should study diligently for tests.*

The pronoun *they* is plural, but *one* is singular. The reader has to guess: Is the author speaking about a group or an individual? Correcting shifts in pronouns means being aware of whether the subject you're replacing is singular or plural, masculine or feminine. The pronoun *one* is often at the root of the problem. It's often easiest to keep pronouns from shifting by replacing one or more of them with more specific words. Here are a couple of examples:

> **Instead of:** *If one is careful, they can avoid additional cable television fees.*
> **Write:** *If cable television subscribers are careful, they can avoid additional fees.*

> **Instead of:** *We asked about interest rates for our mortgage and found out you could lock in at any time.*
> **Write:** *We asked about interest rates for our mortgage, and found out we could lock in at any time.*

Active or Passive Voice

The third type of shift occurs when moving incorrectly from the active to the passive voice, or vice versa. In the active voice, the subject of the sentence performs the action; in the passive voice, the subject receives the action. Keep in mind that in most situations, the active voice is preferred. To correct the shift, change the passive part of the sentence to match the active one. In the following example, the first part of the sentence is written in the active voice; the subject (*Lea*) performs the action (*bought*). However, in the second part, the subject (*it*, or *the sushi*) receives the action (*was eaten*):

> *Lea bought the sushi, and it was eaten by her children.*

To continue the active voice, the sentence should be corrected to read:

> *Lea bought the sushi, and her children ate it.*

Dangling and Misplaced Modifiers

Dangling and misplaced modifiers, though sometimes difficult to recognize, are easily fixed by rearranging word order. A dangling modifier is a phrase or clause, using a verb ending in *-ing*, that does not refer to the subject of the sentence it modifies.

> **Instead of:** *While working on his English assignment, Tony's computer crashed.* (Was the computer working on the assignment?)
> **Write:** *While Tony was working on his English assignment, his computer crashed.*

Note that correcting a dangling modifier involves adding and/or rearranging the words in a sentence to make the meaning clear.

> **Instead of:** *Having been recently fixed, Pedro was able to use the bicycle pump this morning.* (Was Pedro recently fixed?)
> **Write:** *Since the bicycle pump was recently fixed, Pedro was able to use it this morning.*

Misplaced Modifiers

A misplaced modifier is a word or phrase that describes something but is in the wrong place in the sentence. It isn't dangling and no extra words are needed; the modifier is just in the wrong place. The danger of misplaced modifiers, as with dangling modifiers, is that they confuse meaning. Here's an example:

> *I had to have the cafeteria unlocked meeting with student government this morning.*

Did the cafeteria meet with student government? To say exactly what is meant, the modifying phrase *meeting with student government this morning* should be moved to the beginning of the sentence.

> *Meeting with student government this morning, I had to have the cafeteria unlocked.*

Unclear Pronoun References

Recall that pronouns, such as *me, you, he,* and *she,* replace nouns. But when it's not clear what noun the pronoun has replaced or refers to, the meaning of the sentence can get confused. For example:

I went to school every day with Ted and Fred, and we took his car.

Whose car? *His* could mean either Ted's or Fred's. The writer needs to use a proper name instead of the pronoun in order to eliminate the possibility of misunderstanding. Correct it this way: *I went to school every day with Ted and Fred, and we took Ted's car.*

Here's another example:

They considered publishing our poems in the anthology.

Using a vague *they* when there are specific people behind an action is another common pronoun error. In this case, though, the writer doesn't know exactly who those people are. However, even without that information, the sentence can be revised to be more precise: *The publishing company considered publishing our poems in their anthology.*

Here are a few more examples:

Instead of: *They passed new environmental legislation yesterday.*
Write: *The State Senate passed new environmental legislation yesterday.*

Instead of: *Mr. Jones told James that he had found his missing report.*
Write: *Mr. Jones told James that he had found James's missing report.*

Instead of: *They closed the movie theater after they discovered several fire code violations.*
Write: *The owners of the movie theater closed their doors after they discovered several fire code violations.*

Punctuation of Complex Sentences

Varying sentence structures in an SAT essay isn't optional. It's one of five elements scorers are looking for. While including some short and some long sentences does count as variety, there's a more interesting—and eye-catching—way to achieve the kind of diversity that gets you a higher score.

Note the difference between the following two sentences:

> *In his research laboratory in Menlo Park, New Jersey, he invented the phonograph, made the electric lightbulb, and started the motion picture industry.*

> *In his research laboratory (which was located in Menlo Park, New Jersey), he developed some of his most famous inventions: the phonograph, the electric lightbulb, and the motion picture industry.*

The addition of parentheses and a colon takes a straightforward sentence and makes it into one that's more complex—and more interesting. (Note the dash in the previous sentence: It's another great way to add variety and emphasis to your sentences.) You no doubt learned about these punctuation marks in elementary school, so here we'll review them only in terms of how their use helps you improve your SAT essay.

The Colon

Colons can be used to introduce a list when the clause before the colon can stand as a complete sentence on its own.

> **Incorrect:** *The classes he signed up for include: geometry, physics, American literature, and religion.*
> **Correct:** *He signed up for four classes: geometry, physics, American literature, and religion.*

Colons can also be used for a restatement or elaboration of the previous clause.

> **Incorrect:** *Edison was a prolific inventor: He also lived in New Jersey.*
> **Correct:** *Edison was a prolific inventor: He created the electric lightbulb, the phonograph, and many other useful items.*

> **Incorrect:** *Picasso painted* Guernica *in 1937: He was from Spain.*
> **Correct:** *Picasso was inspired to paint* Guernica *in 1937: His work was inspired by the recent destruction of the Spanish city by German bombers.*

Colons are an important addition to persuasive essays because they sound authoritative. They present information more confidently and forcefully than if the sentence were divided by other types of punctuation marks. Consider the following:

> *The effects of climate change are profound: Ice caps are melting and sea levels are rising.*

> *The effects of climate change are profound. Ice caps are melting and sea levels are rising.*

The first example conveys a tone of "I know what is happening, and I am going to tell you." It sounds more convincing and—especially when used in your introductory paragraph—establishes your point of view with greater strength.

The Semicolon

Semicolons are used to separate independent clauses and to separate the items in a list when those items contain commas.

Here's an example of using a semicolon to join independent clauses without a conjunction:

> *Hawthorne wrote* The Scarlet Letter *in 1850; it's one of his most famous works.*

Here's an example of using a semicolon to join independent clauses that contain commas (it may be used even if the clauses are joined by a conjunction):

> *The characters are a product of their Boston, Massachusetts environment; but two of them are able to rise beyond the strict, Puritanical, and stifling society.*

Here's an example of using a semicolon to join independent clauses that are connected with a conjunctive adverb that expresses a relationship between clauses:

> *As the Great Depression deepened, a drought spread across the Plains; therefore, crops were destroyed and many farmers lost their jobs.*

Semicolons may also be used to separate items in a series that contain commas. Here are examples of using a semicolon to show which sets of items go together:

The climate change subcommittee met on Saturday, January 10; Tuesday, April 14; and Thursday, October 11.

Nathaniel Hawthorne lived in Salem, Massachusetts; Liverpool, England; and Concord, Massachusetts.

Parentheses

Use parentheses to set off information that either clarifies or is used as an aside. (Think of asides as any clause or phrase that could begin with *By the way*.) Parentheses are especially useful for breaking up sentences in body paragraphs.

The Smoot-Hawley Act (also known as the Tariff Act of 1930) contributed to the length and severity of the Great Depression.

Roger Chillingworth (Hester Prynne's husband in The Scarlet Letter*) had an outward appearance that matched his inner deformities.*

Dashes

Dashes are used for emphasis and strike an authoritative tone. You can also add them to set off information that contains one or more internal commas or is lengthy or abrupt. One well-placed dash in either your introduction or conclusion can be an effective way to add weight to your point of view. It shows confidence. But if they're used incorrectly or too frequently, dashes make your writing appear sloppy. Stick to the one dash (or set of dashes) rule per essay.

All of his major inventions—the lightbulb, the phonograph, and motion pictures—helped to make Thomas Edison one of the greatest inventors of the modern age.

Picasso's most famous mural—Guernica—is still celebrated as an anti-war message over 70 years after he painted it.

Dashes may also be used at the end of a list of items to highlight their commonality or focus attention on one aspect of those items. Remember that a colon introduces a list (the list is the second part of the sentence). Be certain the text following the dash is an independent clause.

> *Hester Prynne, Arthur Dimmesdale, and Roger Chillingworth—these characters exemplify the strains of Puritan society.*

> *Rising ocean temperatures, more severe weather patterns, melting ice caps— what do the effects of climate change have to do with man's activities?*

Spelling

Some people seem to have inherited good spelling genes. However, if you don't fall into that category, there are a number of basic rules and techniques you can learn to improve your ability to spell.

Five Basic Spelling Rules

1. **I before E:** This rule is familiar to most spellers, but they don't always follow it: *I before E except after C, or when sounding like A as in neighbor or weigh.* That's why *convenient, grievance,* and *lenient* are always on lists of commonly misspelled words.
   - After C: *ceiling, conceit, conceive, deceit, deceive, perceive, receipt, receive.*
   - When sounding like A: *beige, eight, freight, neighbor, sleigh, vein, weigh, weigh, feint.*

   The rule has exceptions (all rules do, and you have to learn them along with the rules!): *conscience, counterfeit, either, foreign, forfeit, height, leisure, neither, science, seize, seizure, species, sufficient, weird*

2. **Doubling final consonants:** Final consonants are doubled when adding a suffix in the following situations:
   - When the ending begins with a vowel (*-ing, -ed, -age, -er, -ence, -ance,* and *-al*)*: hitter, occurrence, stoppage, running.*
   - When the last syllable of the word (before the suffix) is accented and ends in a single consonant preceded by a single vowel: *beginning, incurred, transmittal.*

3. **Dealing with final Es:** There are several possibilities when adding a suffix to a word ending with a silent *e*:

- When adding a suffix that begins with a vowel (*-able, -ing, -ed, -er*), drop the silent *e*: *advancing, larger, movable.*
- Exception: When a final *e* is preceded by a soft *g* or *c*, or a long *o*, the *e* is kept to maintain proper pronunciation: *courageous* (the *g* would have a hard sound if the *e* was dropped), *hopeful* (the *o* would have a short sound if the *e* was dropped), *changeable, noticeable.*
- When adding a suffix that begins with a consonant (*-ful, -less, -ly, -ment, -ness*), keep the final *e*: *amusement, suspenseful, likeness.*
- If a final silent *e* is preceded by another vowel, drop the *e* when adding any ending: *Argue* becomes *argument* or *argued*; *true* becomes *truly.*

4. **Forming plurals:** Plurals are formed in several ways:

- Add an *s* to most words: *chairs, monkeys, rodeos.*
- Add an *es* to words ending in *x, s, sh,* or *ch: churches, foxes, dishes.*
- When a word ends in a consonant plus *y,* change *y* to *ie* and add *s*: *babies, enemies, discrepancies.*
- Add *es* to nouns ending in a long *o* preceded by a consonant (other than musical terms): *buffaloes, embargoes, tomatoes, heroes, mosquitoes, dominoes, volcanoes, potatoes* (but *pianos, sopranos, solos*).
- For many words ending in *f* or *fe,* change *f* or *fe* to *v* and add *s* or *es*: *calves, elves, knives, leaves, lives, loaves, thieves, wives, wolves.*

5. **-cede, -ceed, and –sede:** Only one English word (*supersede*) ends in *-sede.* Only three (*exceed, proceed,* and *succeed*) end in *-ceed.* All others use *-cede.*

The 150 Most Commonly Misspelled Words

Use this list as the basis for starting one of your own. Circle each word that you usually misspell. Write or type your short list on a sheet of paper. Keep it available for quick reference when you're writing, and add other words that you find especially troublesome.

absence	acknowledgment	alleged
abundance	acquaintance	ambiguous
accidentally	aggravate	analysis
accommodate	alibi	annual

argument	discrepancy	interference
awkward	eighth	interrupt
basically	eligible	jealousy
boundary	embarrass	jewelry
bulletin	equivalent	judgment
calendar	euphoria	leisure
canceled	existence	length
cannot	exuberance	lenient
cemetery	feasible	liaison
coincidence	February	lieutenant
collectible	fifth	lightning
committee	forcibly	loophole
comparative	forfeit	losing
completely	formerly	maintenance
condemn	fourth	maneuver
congratulations	fulfill	mathematics
conscientious	grateful	millennium
consistent	grievance	minuscule
convenient	guarantee	miscellaneous
correspondence	guidance	misspell
deceive	harass	negotiable
definitely	hindrance	ninth
dependent	ideally	occasionally
depot	implement	occurred
descend	independence	omission
desperate	indispensable	opportunity
development	inoculate	outrageous
dilemma	insufficient	pamphlet

parallel	receipt	separate
perceive	receive	souvenir
permanent	recommend	specifically
perseverance	reference	sufficient
personnel	referred	supersede
possess	regardless	temperament
potato	relevant	temperature
precede	religious	truly
preferred	remembrance	twelfth
prejudice	reservoir	ubiquitous
prevalent	responsible	unanimous
privilege	restaurant	usually
procedure	rhythm	usurp
proceed	ridiculous	vacuum
prominent	roommate	vengeance
pronunciation	scary	visible
quandary	scissors	Wednesday
questionnaire	secretary	wherever

The best way to remember how to spell the words on your personal "most missed" list is to memorize them. Here are three approaches:

1. **Create mnemonics.** You might remember how to spell *separate* by recalling that it contains *a rat. Cemetery* has three *e*s in it, as in *eeek*. The final vowel in *stationery* is an *e*, as in *envelope*. Creating mnemonics is a great way to improve your spelling.

2. **Organize and reorganize your list of misspelled words.** Group words with the same beginnings or endings, with double vowels, or with double consonants. Come up with three different ways to organize your words.

3. **Take a traditional spelling test.** Give your list to a friend. As he or she reads the words aloud, write them down. Create a shorter list of only those words you misspelled on the test, and work on memorizing those.

CHAPTER

8

THE 25-MINUTE PRACTICE SESSION

The final step in preparing for the SAT essay is to practice. You've already worked on the planning step—those first critical minutes in which you respond to the assignment and choose the examples and evidence to support your point of view. Here, you'll hone your ability to write a complete essay in 25 minutes.

For each session, you may use a blank piece of paper for planning. During the SAT, you'll be able to use your test booklet. While the section to write your essay is a straight 48 lines, know that the answer sheet on which you write will be divided evenly into two pages—so you'll always be aware of how much more you need to write. (Recall that your goal is at least one and a half pages.)

Once you're finished with an essay, use the guided self-assessment to determine what worked and where you could improve. You might decide you need a review of transition words and their use or that you need more flexible predetermined content. It's also helpful to ask someone with a strong grasp of grammar and usage to read your essay; finding your own errors can be difficult. After a few practice sessions, your results may indicate that you're test-ready.

One final word of advice: Don't try to do more than one practice session in a day. Take the time to absorb what you learned in the assessment, and adjust and/or review as necessary before trying another complete essay. As you learned in Chapter 1, the SAT essay is much like a math problem. Once you've got a formula that works, you can apply it to any prompt.

Session One

Prompt:

When we witness an injustice or the violation of a principle, anger can give us the courage to act, not react. Productive anger can be a guide to appropriate, powerful, and healing action. All the political and social movements of our time are rooted in anger, including the struggle against apartheid, the fight for civil rights, and many environmental and animal protection initiatives. The founders of these movements experienced healthy anger against conditions they considered to be unjust and unacceptable.

—Adapted from *The Ultimate Guide to Transforming Anger*,
by JANE MIDDELTON-MOZ, LISA TENER, and PEACO TODD
(Health Communications, 2004)

Assignment:

Can anger be used for positive results? Organize and compose an essay that establishes your viewpoint on this issue. Substantiate it with examples and evidence derived from what you have read, studied, experienced, or observed.

_____

_____

_____

_____

_____

_____

_____

Evaluation

For all criteria, note whether your effort was (1) weak, (2) adequate, or (3) good to great. Answer only those that are applicable.

Planning

Met time restriction (4–6 minutes)	1	2	3
Located heartbeat words	1	2	3
Chose quality examples	1	2	3
Responded to assignment	1	2	3

Thesis Statement

Used heartbeat words	1	2	3
Argument based on best examples	1	2	3

Introductory Paragraph

Used a hook	1	2	3
Briefly introduced examples	1	2	3

Body Paragraphs

Used one example per paragraph, mentioned in your introduction	1	2	3
Used heartbeat words	1	2	3
Used details and evidence to support each example	1	2	3
Logically and smoothly progressed from one idea to another	1	2	3
Used at least two types of sentence structures	1	2	3
Long enough to fill at least one page (more than one total with introduction)	1	2	3

Conclusion

Included a reworked thesis statement	1	2	3
Was at least two sentences long	1	2	3
Ended with a question, quote, or analogy	1	2	3

Overall

Met time restriction	1	2	3
Showed good grasp of grammar, vocabulary, and mechanics	1	2	3

Session Two

Prompt:

> *The youth of today is not the youth of twenty years ago. This much any elderly person would say, at any point in history, and think it was both new and true. Youth seem to want to be that which society tells them not to be: in this they conform.*
>
> —Adapted from *Identity*:
> *Youth and Crisis*, by ERIK ERIKSON
> (W.W. Norton & Company, 1968)

Assignment:

> *Are youth today less conformist than they once were? Organize and compose an essay that establishes your viewpoint on this issue. Substantiate it with examples and evidence derived from what you have read, studied, experienced, or observed.*

_____

_____

_____

_____

_____

_____

_____

_____

_____

Evaluation

For all criteria, note whether your effort was (1) weak, (2) adequate, or (3) good to great. Answer only those that are applicable.

Planning

Met time restriction (4–6 minutes)	1	2	3
Located heartbeat words	1	2	3
Chose quality examples	1	2	3
Responded to assignment	1	2	3

Thesis Statement

Used heartbeat words	1	2	3
Argument based on best examples	1	2	3

Introductory Paragraph

Used a hook	1	2	3
Briefly introduced examples	1	2	3

Body Paragraphs

Used one example per paragraph, mentioned in your introduction	1	2	3
Used heartbeat words	1	2	3
Used details and evidence to support each example	1	2	3
Logically and smoothly progressed from one idea to another	1	2	3
Used at least two types of sentence structures	1	2	3
Long enough to fill at least one page (more than one total with introduction)	1	2	3

Conclusion

Included a reworked thesis statement	1	2	3
Was at least two sentences long	1	2	3
Ended with a question, quote, or analogy	1	2	3

Overall

Met time restriction	1	2	3
Showed good grasp of grammar, vocabulary, and mechanics	1	2	3

Session Three

Prompt:

The worship of artists as heroes is both commonplace and misguided. Why does the creation of a work of art impose on the artist the obligation to lead an exemplary life? The artists have fulfilled their contracts with us by producing work that gives us pleasure or insight or both. Why hold them to an unwritten morals clause?

—Adapted from "Loves of a Poet,"
by RHONDA KOENIG

Assignment:

Is it valuable to view artists and other public figures as heroes? Organize and compose an essay that establishes your viewpoint on this issue. Substantiate it with examples and evidence derived from what you have read, studied, experienced, or observed.

Evaluation

For all criteria, note whether your effort was (1) weak, (2) adequate, or (3) good to great. Answer only those that are applicable.

Planning

Met time restriction (4–6 minutes)	1	2	3
Located heartbeat words	1	2	3
Chose quality examples	1	2	3
Responded to assignment	1	2	3

Thesis Statement

Used heartbeat words	1	2	3
Argument based on best examples	1	2	3

Introductory Paragraph

Used a hook	1	2	3
Briefly introduced examples	1	2	3

Body Paragraphs

Used one example per paragraph, mentioned in your introduction	1	2	3
Used heartbeat words	1	2	3
Used details and evidence to support each example	1	2	3
Logically and smoothly progressed from one idea to another	1	2	3
Used at least two types of sentence structures	1	2	3
Long enough to fill at least one page (more than one total with introduction)	1	2	3

Conclusion

Included a reworked thesis statement	1	2	3
Was at least two sentences long	1	2	3
Ended with a question, quote, or analogy	1	2	3

Overall

Met time restriction	1	2	3
Showed good grasp of grammar, vocabulary, and mechanics	1	2	3

Session Four

Prompt:

Scholars and researchers have tried to measure the links between intelligence and genius. But intelligence is not enough. Run of the mill physicists have much higher IQs than Nobel Prize–winner Richard Feynman, whom many acknowledge to be the last great American genius. Genius is not about scoring a 2400 on the SATs, mastering ten languages at the age of seven, having an extraordinarily high IQ, or even about being smart. After considerable debate, psychologists reached the conclusion that creativity is not the same as intelligence. An individual can be far more creative than he or she is intelligent, or far more intelligent than creative.

—Adapted from *Cracking Creativity*,
by Michael Michalko (Ten Speed Press, 2001)

Assignment:

Is creativity more important than intelligence? Organize and compose an essay that establishes your viewpoint on this issue. Substantiate it with examples and evidence derived from what you have read, studied, experienced, or observed.

Evaluation

For all criteria, note whether your effort was (1) weak, (2) adequate, or (3) good to great. Answer only those that are applicable.

Planning

Met time restriction (4–6 minutes)	1	2	3
Located heartbeat words	1	2	3
Chose quality examples	1	2	3
Responded to assignment	1	2	3

Thesis Statement

Used heartbeat words	1	2	3
Argument based on best examples	1	2	3

Introductory Paragraph

Used a hook	1	2	3
Briefly introduced examples	1	2	3

Body Paragraphs

Used one example per paragraph, mentioned in your introduction	1	2	3
Used heartbeat words	1	2	3
Used details and evidence to support each example	1	2	3
Logically and smoothly progressed from one idea to another	1	2	3
Used at least two types of sentence structures	1	2	3
Long enough to fill at least one page (more than one total with introduction)	1	2	3

Conclusion

Included a reworked thesis statement	1	2	3
Was at least two sentences long	1	2	3
Ended with a question, quote, or analogy	1	2	3

Overall

Met time restriction	1	2	3
Showed good grasp of grammar, vocabulary, and mechanics	1	2	3

Session Five

Prompt:

Most people acknowledge that they occasionally tell "white lies." They justify their behavior with reasons ranging from protecting others' feelings to saving a life. The common thread in these claims is that telling the truth in certain situations would cause more harm than good. And yet the definition of harm varies greatly.

Assignment:

Is it sometimes better to lie? Organize and compose an essay that establishes your viewpoint on this issue. Substantiate it with examples and evidence derived from what you have read, studied, experienced, or observed.

_____

_____

_____

_____

_____

_____

_____

_____

_____

_____

_____

_____

_____

_____

_____

_____

_____

_____

_____

_____

_____

_____

_____

_____

_____

_____

_____

_____

_____

_____

_____

_____

_____

Evaluation

For all criteria, note whether your effort was (1) weak, (2) adequate, or (3) good to great. Answer only those that are applicable.

Planning

Met time restriction (4–6 minutes)	1	2	3
Located heartbeat words	1	2	3
Chose quality examples	1	2	3
Responded to assignment	1	2	3

Thesis Statement

Used heartbeat words	1	2	3
Argument based on best examples	1	2	3

Introductory Paragraph

Used a hook	1	2	3
Briefly introduced examples	1	2	3

Body Paragraphs

Used one example per paragraph, mentioned in your introduction	1	2	3
Used heartbeat words	1	2	3
Used details and evidence to support each example	1	2	3
Logically and smoothly progressed from one idea to another	1	2	3
Used at least two types of sentence structures	1	2	3
Long enough to fill at least one page (more than one total with introduction)	1	2	3

Conclusion

Included a reworked thesis statement	1	2	3
Was at least two sentences long	1	2	3
Ended with a question, quote, or analogy	1	2	3

Overall

Met time restriction	1	2	3
Showed good grasp of grammar, vocabulary, and mechanics	1	2	3
Was at least one and a half pages long (used at least 36 lines)	1	2	3

What's Next?

Review the evaluations for each exercise. Did you see a trend of improvement, or are there areas that still need work? We'll pay particular attention to the five key areas scorers are looking for (the list is in Chapter 1 on page 4). Here are the steps you may need to take to continue building your essay writing skills.

If you couldn't plan your essay in four to six minutes and/or couldn't complete the essay in 25 minutes: What step or steps took longer than your budgeted allowance (4–6 minutes planning, 14–17 drafting, 2–3 editing)? Why? Still having trouble planning? Reread Chapter 3, and then find practice prompts (listed in the appendix). Complete at least five more planning sessions, concentrating only on the step(s) that took longest to complete. Run out of time for a conclusion? Have a line handy to toss in. Something like "It is for these reasons that (insert variation on thesis statement)" is much better than nothing. Practice writing such lines alone, using a couple of the essays you completed in this chapter.

If your introduction didn't use a hook or adequately mention your examples: First, remember than a hook is optional. While it is an element that can take a good essay to great, it doesn't work for every writer. If the hook isn't working, stick with your thesis statement. It's a solid start. If you said too much or too little about the examples you developed in your body paragraphs, edit that introduction. Rework it until you're satisfied, then try writing a few more introductions (after planning an essay) using online sample prompts.

If your essay didn't use the heartbeat words often enough: Recall that this is a strategy designed to show the clear focus that your scorers are looking for. Practice on five assignments at the end of Chapter 3. Circle these words boldly. For each assignment, write a few sentences that you might use in an essay on the assignment—and use the heartbeat words in each.

If your body paragraphs weren't detailed enough: First alert! This is one of the five most important elements of your essay. Your examples, which are explained through details and evidence, are what help you develop your point of view. Go back to some of the essays you wrote and brainstorm more details in the margins. You might find that one or more of your content topics need further research.

If you gave yourself a low mark for organization: Alert number two! Review the list of transition words and explanations of their use on page 67 in Chapter 5. Copy the words and keep them handy as you write one of the additional essays in the appendix. Your fix might be as simple as using *For example* in your first body paragraph and *Another example* in your second. Even if the connection between the two isn't strong, confident words like these will hint to your reader that you are presenting a logical argument.

If you didn't show enough variety with your sentence structure: Alert number three! Again, this is a critical mark to hit. Review the section in Chapter 5 on Sentence Structure (page 73), and then rework the body paragraphs of some of your essays to add greater variety.

If you made multiple mistakes in grammar and/or mechanics or if you didn't use any words that could be considered part of a college-level vocabulary: Final alert! Carefully review Chapters 6 and 7; they address the issues you need to know—now. Do you remember the words you brainstormed in the exercise on page 69 in Chapter 5? Review them, and start memorizing the vocabulary list in the appendix.

If your essay was not at least 36 lines long: While this is not clearly stated as a scoring criterion, the importance of length can't be overstated, especially if you're aiming for a score of 11 or 12. Review the high scoring sample essays on www.collegeboard.com, and you'll notice that they're all at least one and a half pages long. Check your essays carefully to see where you could have added information. Rework a few of them, including enough material to get the right length, and then practice with some of the assignments in the appendix or online. Also consider the size of your handwriting and indentations—they can be adjusted (within reason) to achieve greater length too.

In these online essay exercises, the emphasis is on focus and organization. Your essays should address the prompts and be logically organized, with ideas flowing easily from one to another.

To complete these online activities, go to the **Additional Online Practice** page on page 165 and follow the instructions.

Once you have logged in, click **Start** under one of the prompts offered.

When completing each essay, click in the empty white box under the instructions and begin to type your sample essay response to the prompt. Periodically click **Save** to make sure that your work is not erased!

When you are finished writing each essay, click **Next Page**. If you'd like to review your work before having it scored, click **Back**. If you are happy with your essay and feel it is complete, click **Score My Test**. You will receive an automatic essay score from 1–6. Click on the link titled **View Scoring Guide** to get a better sense of the criteria used to evaluate your essay.

In addition to getting a sense of the mechanical aspects of your essay, take another look at what you have written by clicking on **View Essay**.

As you check your essay scores, note especially the organization and support results. Your numbers were based on focus, logical order, seamless flow of ideas, development, and relevance. Reread your essays with those characteristics in mind. If you scored less than 6 on either organization or support, review your essays and check for the following:

- Do you have a clear thesis (your most important responsibility)?
- Do your major points describe your responsibility?
- Are those points supported by examples (think *show* rather than *tell*)?
- Is the organization logical, or should parts of the essay be moved, developed more fully, or removed?
- Did you use transitions to move from one idea to another?

Consider rewriting your essays to improve on any weaknesses, taking note of the importance of focus and organization.

SAMPLE ESSAYS, SCORES, AND ANALYSES

The essays in this chapter were written using two of the sample assignments in Chapter 8. To learn from these examples, it's important to pay careful attention to the analysis that follows each. Analyses are based on the College Board's Essay Scoring Guide (found at www.collegeboard.com) and emphasize the attributes that readers look for in determining their holistic scores.

Essay 1

Prompt (for Essays 1, 2, and 3):

When we witness an injustice or the violation of a principle, anger can give us the courage to act, not react. Productive anger can be a guide to appropriate, powerful, and healing action. All the political and social movements of our time are rooted in anger, including the struggle against apartheid, the fight for civil rights, and many environmental and animal protection initiatives. The founders of these movements experienced healthy anger against conditions they considered to be unjust and unacceptable.

—Adapted from *The Ultimate Guide to Transforming Anger*,
by JANE MIDDELTON-MOZ, LISA TENER, and PEACO TODD
(Health Communications, 2004)

Assignment (for Essays 1, 2, and 3):

Can anger be used for positive results? Organize and compose an essay that establishes your viewpoint on this issue. Substantiate it with examples and evidence derived from what you have read, studied, experienced, or observed.

Can anger ever produce positive results? The lives of some very famous people indicate that it can. Anger can promote creativity. In the case of Mrs. Nancy Edison, Thomas Edison's mother, it caused her to find a better solution to her son's inadequate schooling. In other cases, like that of Picasso, anger was the spark behind one of his greatest works of art, a mural whose meaning still resonates strongly today.

American inventor Thomas Edison (1847–1931) has been described as more responsible than anyone else for creating the modern world. In his research laboratory in Menlo Park, New Jersey, he invented the phonograph, made the electric lightbulb, and started the motion picture industry. However, his success had nothing to do with his schooling. In fact, the young Edison attended school for just three months—when his inattention and constant questioning caused his teacher to say he was slow, his mother removed him from the school. Nancy Edison taught her son at home, encouraging him to read and experiment. Edison later noted, "My mother was the making of me." Her anger at his treatment in school caused her to take charge of his education and as a result helped to foster one of the great geniuses in our country's history.

Just a few years after Edison's death on another continent, anger created another positive result. In 1937, Pablo Picasso agreed to paint a mural for the World's Fair in Paris. But he had a difficult time choosing a subject. Then, German bombers attacked the city of Guernica in his native Spain. Although he once said art should not be political, Picasso was so angry that he chose the violent attack as the subject of his mural. Guernica shows the brutality of war in stark black and white, depicting innocent victims that include children and animals. The painting, created out of anger, still serves today as a visual reminder of the devastation and violence of war. The painter noted famously that "Art enables us to see the truth."

By allowing anger to motivate us—as opposed to silencing or just frustrating us—we can achieve positive results. Just as a great leader, when he or she sees injustice, is inspired to seek change for the betterment of people, so too can all people use their anger to give them energy to make things better.

Your Notes and Reactions

_____

_____

_____

_____

_____

_____

_____

_____

_____

Score and Analysis

This essay received a 12. It demonstrates the kind of clear and consistent mastery required to achieve the highest possible score from both readers. Overall, it creates a strong argument regarding the benefits of anger, using appropriate examples that are rich in detail. Recall the five areas scorers are evaluating to determine their holistic score:

1. **Developed a point of view supported by appropriate examples and evidence?**
   To earn a score of 12, essays must demonstrate outstanding critical thinking. This piece does that by focusing on two excellent examples of positive results stemming from anger. It clearly links Edison and Picasso to the assignment through the use of heartbeat words (*anger* and *positive*)—these words are used 12 times in four paragraphs. Each example is then developed with ample evidence. The Edison story (which begins with the two predetermined background sentences) explains clearly how his situation at school angered his mother, what her subsequent actions were, and how they created a positive result. The Picasso example also contains the details needed for

development. It includes a number of themes, including his delay in choosing a subject, his previous belief that art should not be political, his reaction to the bombing, and his depiction of it.

2. **Wrote with a clear focus, transitioned smoothly from one point to the next?** The heartbeat words and choice of examples demonstrate a clear focus on the assignment. The essay is also coherent—it does not veer off course; every sentence contributes to the argument. Note the interesting transition used by this writer: Because she knows when Edison died and when Picasso painted *Guernica*, she was able to tie these two examples together not just thematically, but also chronologically (*Just a few years after Edison's death, on another continent, anger created another positive result*).

3. **Avoided errors in grammar, mechanics, and usage?** The essay shows a skillful use of language. The introduction begins with a question, and the conclusion contains an analogy. It is also free of grammar, mechanics, and usage errors.

4. **Varied sentence structure?** Simple, complex, long, and short sentences are used in the essay.

5. **Showed evidence of a varied and intelligent vocabulary?** Words such as *resonates*, *foster*, and *depicting* demonstrate a varied and accurate use of vocabulary.

Essay 2

Anger can produce positive results. The lives of some very famous people indicate that it can promote creativity. In some cases, that could mean better problem solving. In others, great works of art can be made.

Thomas Edison (1847–1931) has been described as more responsible than anyone else for creating the modern world. In his research laboratory in Menlo Park, New Jersey, he invented the phonograph, made the electric lightbulb, and started the motion picture industry. But his success wasn't because of his education. It was because of his mother. Mrs. Edison was angered by the way her son was treated by his teacher so she took him out of school and taught him herself. He became a famous inventor—all because of his mother's decision.

Pablo Picasso is another example of someone who had positive results from his anger. In 1937 he painted a mural for the Worlds Fair in Paris. It depicts the aftermath of the German bombing of Guernica, a city in his native Spain. Picasso was so angry about the bombing that he used it as the subject of his painting, even though he once said art should never be political. Guernica shows the violence and brutality of war, and it is still considered one of the most powerful anti-war paintings in the history of art. As Picasso said, "Art enables us to see the truth."

These two examples clearly show that anger can produce the result of creativity. Whether in the form of a better solution to a problem, or an expressive work of art, anger can be a positive force.

Your Notes and Reactions

_____

_____

_____

_____

_____

_____

Score and Analysis

This essay received a 10, demonstrating reasonably consistent mastery.

1. **Developed a point of view supported by appropriate examples and evidence?** Strong critical thinking is evident in the selection of the Edison and Picasso examples, and the link to the creativity that can result from anger, making anger a positive force. The essay uses heartbeat words (*anger* and *positive*) nine times in four paragraphs to show the link between each example and the assignment. Each example is supported with evidence, but notice that the Picasso paragraph is better developed. The Edison story (which begins with the two predetermined background sentences) states that his situation at school angered his mother, but doesn't explain why. The last two sentences are also unsupported statements. The Picasso example contains more pertinent and thorough details. It includes a number of themes, including his delay in choosing a subject, his previous belief that art should not be political, his reaction to the bombing, and his depiction of it in his painting.

2. **Wrote with a clear focus, transitioned smoothly from one point to the next?** The heartbeat words and choice of examples demonstrate a clear focus on the assignment. The essay is also coherent—the examples are briefly mentioned in the introduction, and there is a clear link between them (both illustrate the creativity that can result from anger).

3. **Avoided errors in grammar, mechanics, and usage?** The essay shows a facility in the use of language. It is nearly free of grammar, mechanics, and usage errors.

4. **Varied sentence structure?** Simple, complex, long, and short sentences are used in the essay.

5. **Showed evidence of a varied and intelligent vocabulary?** Words such as *brutality*, *native*, and *expressive* are evidence of an appropriate vocabulary.

Essay 3

Some people think that anger is just a negative emotion and it should always be held under control. But sometimes anger can be used for positive results. In these cases, it shows that it was well to not resist feeling anger but to use it for positive purposes.

This lesson is clear when you look at the life of inventor Thomas Edison, who is known as more responsible than anyone else for creating the modern world. In his research laboratory in New Jersey, he invented many things. But as a child, his life was anything but successful. His mother didn't like his teacher. She got so angry she took him out of school and home schooled him instead.

Another example of the positive results from anger was seen in my school this year. In student government there were a lot of students who had good ideas about a service project for our school. It was really hard to decide what to do, and people got very angry when they had to defend their ideas. But finally when we came to a decision, it was a blend of a couple of different ideas, which shows that the anger produced a positive result.

As you can see from these two examples, anger can produce positive results.

Your Notes and Reactions

_____

_____

_____

_____

_____

Score and Analysis

This essay received an 8. It demonstrates adequate mastery, with some strengths and a few weaknesses.

1. **Developed a point of view supported by appropriate examples and evidence?** Both examples support the thesis that sometimes anger can produce positive results. Notice that the writer remembered some background information for the first example and used an appropriate personal experience for his second example. However, neither example is well developed. There are not enough details or evidence to strongly support the position. There is too much telling and not enough showing (see Chapter 5, page 72).

2. **Wrote with a clear focus, transitioned smoothly from one point to the next?** While the essay isn't well developed, it does repeat the heartbeat words often enough to demonstrate focus. The use of the transition word *another* lets the reader know that the writer is moving from the first to the second example; however the lack of indentation makes it unclear if a new paragraph is beginning (this also shortens the essay slightly).

3. **Avoided errors in grammar, mechanics, and usage?** The essay shows an inconsistent use of language. It has some grammar, mechanics, and usage errors.

4. **Varied sentence structure?** There is some variation in sentence structure.

5. **Showed evidence of a varied and intelligent vocabulary?** The essay exhibits a generally appropriate vocabulary but does not display particularly thoughtful word choice.

Essay 4

Prompt (for Essays 4, 5, and 6):

The worship of artists as heroes is both commonplace and misguided. Why does the creation of a work of art impose on the artist the obligation to lead an exemplary life? The artists have fulfilled their contracts with us by producing work that gives us pleasure or insight or both. Why hold them to an unwritten morals clause?

—Adapted from "Loves of a Poet," by RHONDA KOENIG

Assignment (for Essays 4, 5, and 6):

Is it valuable to view artists and other public figures as heroes? Organize and compose an essay that establishes your viewpoint on this issue. Substantiate it with examples and evidence derived from what you have read, studied, experienced, or observed.

There have been heroes throughout recorded history. From the hero cults of ancient Greece to present day movie stars, people seem to need to look up to, and even to worship, those deemed to be of a higher caliber. However, there is a serious downside to valuing an individual as a hero—both to the person and to the worshippers. Heroes, because they're human and therefore flawed, can never live up to the image. Heroes are doomed to either pretend to be better than they truly are, or show themselves honestly (or be found out) and fall from grace. Those who worship them view life through black and white lenses. To them, everyone is all good or all bad, and this view keeps them from seeing the truth about anything or anyone.

In *The Scarlet Letter* (1850), Nathaniel Hawthorne illustrates the ill effects of hero worship in the character of Arthur Dimmesdale. This minister is respected by his congregation as a pure and saintly man of God. However, Dimmesdale is also the lover of the married Hester Prynne, and therefore guilty of the sin of adultery. He works very hard to keep his relationship to Hester, who is severely punished by her community, a secret. The more Dimmesdale leads a double life, wearing "one face to himself, and another to the multitude," the more he deteriorates physically. Hawthorne describes him as emaciated and sickly, and by the end of the novel, when he finally reveals that he is not the hero they thought he was, the health effects of his double life cause his death.

However, those who worshipped him, even in the end, fail to understand this significant point. The Puritans' strict moral code and intolerance for dissent of any kind make them incapable of seeing the truth. Throughout the novel, Hawthorne describes the way that his followers, by holding him up as a hero, misinterpret Dimmesdale. As he becomes more frail, they believe it is a sign of his sacrifice. As his sermons become more meaningful, they attribute his "gift" to God, when instead his words are inspired by his own inner wrestling with his sinfulness. The most important misinterpretation comes when Dimmesdale is on the scaffold with Hester, and a meteor seems to make the letter "A" in the sky. Dimmesdale sees it as a sign that he should be wearing the letter with Hester, while the community believes it stands for "Angel." In the end, the Puritans, although they have been given ample evidence to the contrary, still find value in the strict moral code that deems people either saints or sinners. They are stuck in their black and white world that cannot see the truth.

Hawthorne showed us, over 150 years ago, that it is not always valuable to hold people up to be heroes and that it can be dangerous both to the worshipped and the worshipper. If we heed his lesson, seeing shades of grey rather than black and white, we can move a step closer to living in truth.

Your Notes and Reactions

Score and Analysis

This essay received a 12. It demonstrates the kind of clear and consistent mastery required to achieve the highest possible score from both readers. Overall, it creates a strong argument that there is a serious downside to valuing an individual as a hero—both to the person and to the worshippers. It explores this point of view through an in-depth discussion of *The Scarlet Letter* that is developed in great detail.

1. **Developed a point of view supported by appropriate examples and evidence?** The writer shows outstanding critical thinking by focusing on two aspects of the novel as they relate to the thesis: the effects of hero worship on Dimmesdale and the effects on his community (because he is a minister, those who hold him up to be a hero can literally be called worshippers). Each example is developed with many details. Dimmesdale's double life and its effects on his health are described, and a quote from the novel is included. The thesis is strongly supported by a description of the various ways his worshippers' blindness to the truth cause them to misinterpret both Dimmesdale and the world around them.

2. **Wrote with a clear focus, transitioned smoothly from one point to the next?** The use of heartbeat words (*value/valuable* and *hero(es)*) helps to establish a link to the assignment throughout the essay; they are used ten times in four paragraphs. Note that only one example, *The Scarlet Letter*, is used; however, the writer is able to argue both points well. The third paragraph provides an interesting transition, concluding a point made in the preceding sentence.

3. **Avoided errors in grammar, mechanics, and usage?** The essay shows a skillful use of language. The introduction begins with a confident statement, and the conclusion offers a suggestion. It is also free of grammar, mechanics, and usage errors.

4. **Varied sentence structure?** Simple, complex, long, and short sentences are used in the essay.

5. **Showed evidence of a varied and intelligent vocabulary?** Words such as *caliber*, *emaciated*, and *dissent* demonstrate a varied and accurate vocabulary.

Essay 5

There is a serious downside to valuing an individual as a hero. Because they're human they can't be perfect, so they can never live up to the image. Heroes either have to pretend to be better than they are, or be honest or get caught and disappoint everyone.

Nathaniel Hawthorne's *The Scarlet Letter* (1850), has the perfect setting to explore the downside of hero worship. The Puritan society of seventeenth century Boston has a strict moral code and intolerance for dissent—everyone sees everything as black or white. You're either pure or a sinner. The minister Arthur Dimmesdale is believed to be pure and saintly but he is really a sinner. Dimmesdale leads a double life, wearing "one face to himself, and another to the multitude," which eventually kills him. But his worshippers never understand that they were wrong to see someone as only good. There are many times in the book where they could see the truth about Dimmesdale but they never do. They always prefer to see everything as black and white.

Tiger Woods recent problems are another example of why it is not valuable to see someone as a hero. He was worshipped by many not just as a great golfer, but as a great man with a beautiful family who had everything going for him. But then the truth came out that he was a person who makes mistakes. This has cost him his family, millions of dollars, and maybe even his career—all because he could not live up to the perfect image everyone had of him.

Hawthorne wrote in *The Scarlet Letter*, "No man, for any considerable period, can wear one face to himself, and another to the multitude, without finally getting bewildered as to which may be true." This is why it is not valuable to hold up people as heroes.

Your Notes and Reactions

_____

_____

_____

_____

_____

Score and Analysis

This essay received an 8. It demonstrates adequate mastery, with some strengths and a few weaknesses.

1. **Developed a point of view supported by appropriate examples and evidence?** Both examples provide strong support for the thesis that there is a serious downside to valuing an individual as a hero. The academic example uses some background information and a quote from the novel, but it lacks detail. The second paragraph is filled with unsupported statements such as *there are many times in the novel when they could see the truth*. Evidence is needed to develop these points fully. The third paragraph uses an appropriate example, but it also lacks detail. The fact that *the truth came out* (which is the point on which the paragraph rests) is not explained. The writer may have assumed that everyone knows this information, but on the SAT Essay, readers are looking for details and evidence—not unsupported statements.

2. **Wrote with a clear focus, transitioned smoothly from one point to the next?** While the essay isn't well developed, it does repeat the heartbeat words often enough to demonstrate focus. Every paragraph is clearly linked, and the use of the transition word *another* lets the reader know that the writer is moving from the first to the second example.

3. **Avoided errors in grammar, mechanics, and usage?** The essay shows an inconsistent use of language. It has some grammar, mechanics, and usage errors.

4. **Varied sentence structure?** There is some variation in sentence structure.

5. **Showed evidence of a varied and intelligent vocabulary?** The essay exhibits a generally appropriate vocabulary.

Essay 6

It is not good to value people as heroes. People are not as good as you think they are and you will get disappointed when you figure out that they are not who you think they are. It's not fair to them either.

The Scarlet Letter by Nathaniel Hawthorne has a character who is a hero to people. Arthur Dimmesdale is a minister and everyone thinks he is really good. But he is secretly Pearls father. He is a sinner and he feels bad about that. But no one else knows it except Hester and Pearl.

This happened with Tiger Woods too. People looked up to him as if he was perfect, and he made a lot of money through that view of himself. He was not just a great golfer, he was a "clean" guy did not do anything wrong. But then people found out the truth. This of course hurt Tiger, but it also hurt the companies that were using Tiger for their products. They paid him millions of dollars to be the prefect golfer and perfect man but then he wasn't.

It is not valuable to think of people as heros. Arthur Dimmesdale and Tiger Woods prove that. When you see somebody as a hero, you don't see the truth of them, only a perfect image that nobody can really live up to.

Your Notes and Reactions

_____

_____

_____

_____

Score and Analysis

This essay received a 6. It displays developing mastery, with some critical weaknesses.

1. **Developed a point of view supported by appropriate examples and evidence?** Both examples attempt to support the thesis that it is not good to value people as heroes. Neither example is developed well through details or evidence; both body paragraphs are almost all telling with little showing.

2. **Wrote with a clear focus, transitioned smoothly from one point to the next?** While the essay isn't well developed, it is coherent. Repetition of the heartbeat words maintains a focus on the thesis. The transition from the second to third paragraph is adequate (*This happened with Tiger Woods too*).

3. **Avoided errors in grammar, mechanics, and usage?** The essay contains a number of errors.

4. **Varied sentence structure?** There is little variation in sentence structure.

5. **Showed evidence of a varied and intelligent vocabulary?** Vocabulary is very basic.

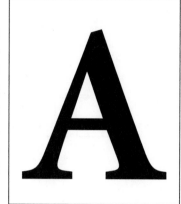

ADDITIONAL ESSAY PRACTICE, SAT VOCABULARY, COLLEGE ADMISSIONS RESOURCES

Five Essay Practice Sessions

Session One

Prompt:

A recent study ranked 178 countries according to levels of happiness reported by their citizens. Respondents chose from a range of determining factors, including education, life expectancy, and income. These three (not in this order) were in fact the most closely correlated with well-being.

Assignment:

Is income more important than any other factor in determining happiness? Organize and compose an essay that establishes your viewpoint on this issue. Substantiate it with examples and evidence derived from what you have read, studied, experienced, or observed.

_____

_____

_____

Session Two

Prompt:

Groups matter. On a practical level, much of the world's work is done by groups. Groups are also the keys to understanding people—why they think, feel, and act the way they do. Human behavior is so often group behavior that people cannot be studied in isolation. All kinds of societies are defined by the small groups that compose them. Societal forces, such as traditions, values, and norms, do not reach directly to individuals, but instead work through the groups to which each individual belongs.

—Adapted from *Group Dynamics*,
by DONELSON R. FORSYTH (1998, Wadsworth)

Assignment:

Are all values group values or do some originate with the individual? Organize and compose an essay that establishes your viewpoint on this issue. Substantiate it with examples and evidence derived from what you have read, studied, experienced, or observed.

Session Three

Prompt:

> *In a literal sense, there is "nothing new under the sun." Every development rests on previous ones. Devices we call new are only combinations of two or more old ones. The originality of inventors lies in seeing relationships that occurred to no one else. That ability is the heart of invention and originality.*
>
> —Adapted from "How to Produce New Ideas,"
> by WEBB GARRISON (*Popular Mechanics*, Vol. 1. No. 3, 1954)

Assignment:

> *Is anything truly original? Organize and compose an essay that establishes your viewpoint on this issue. Substantiate it with examples and evidence derived from what you have read, studied, experienced, or observed.*

Session Four

Prompt:

Scholars and researchers have tried to measure the links between intelligence and genius. But intelligence is not enough. Run of the mill physicists have much higher IQs than Nobel Prize-winner Richard Feynman, whom many acknowledge to be the last great American genius. After considerable debate, they reached the conclusion that creativity is not the same as intelligence. An individual can be far more creative than he or she is intelligent, or far more intelligent than creative.

—Adapted from *Cracking Creativity*,
by Michael Michalko (Ten Speed Press, 2001)

Assignment:

Is creativity more important than intelligence? Organize and compose an essay that establishes your viewpoint on this issue. Substantiate it with examples and evidence derived from what you have read, studied, experienced, or observed.

_____

_____

_____

_____

_____

_____

_____

_____

_____

_____

Session 5

Prompt:

Most people acknowledge that they occasionally tell "white lies." They justify their behavior with reasons ranging from protecting others' feelings to saving a life. The common thread in these claims is that telling the truth in certain situations would bring more harm than good. And yet the definition of harm varies greatly.

Assignment:

Is it sometimes better to lie? Organize and compose an essay that establishes your viewpoint on this issue. Substantiate it with examples and evidence derived from what you have read, studied, experienced, or observed.

SAT Vocabulary

Word	Definition
abide	*v:* to remain or continue; to put up with
acrimony	*n:* bitterness or harshness (describing someone's character)
aesthetic	*a:* relating to beauty
alleviate	*v:* to lessen, ease
amalgam	*n:* a mixture
amorphous	*a:* formless, without definite shape
anecdote	*n:* a story
antithesis	*n:* the opposite of
banal	*a:* overused; repeated too often; trite
benign	*a:* kind; harmless (when used as medical term)
callow	*a:* young, inexperienced, immature
candid	*a:* outspoken, honest, frank
chimerical	*a:* wildly imaginative
consensus	*n:* opinion agreed to by a group
debase	*v:* to lower the quality or value of something; to corrupt
decorous	*a:* dignified; having good manners
digress	*v:* to deviate from or to stray; to depart from the main point in an argument
diminutive	*a:* small
earthy	*a:* natural; uninhibited
ebullient	*a:* enthusiastic, lively
eclectic	*a:* made up of elements from various sources
eminent	*a:* superior; of a higher level; noteworthy
enigmatic	*a:* mysterious
facile	*a:* easy

frenetic	*a:* frantic; wildly excited
futile	*a:* useless; producing no result
gratuitous	*a:* unnecessary
hubris	*n:* excessive pride
impede	*v:* to slow or stop; to act as an obstruction
impudent	*a:* rude, offensive
intemperate	*a:* extreme, unrestrained
invective	*n:* speech that abuses or puts someone down
loathe	*v:* to hate
mundane	*a:* ordinary, boring
orthodox	*a:* following the conventional or approved way (see *unconventional*)
paradox	*a:* a statement that seems to contradict itself but is true
petulant	*a:* extremely irritable or moody
portend	*v:* to warn; to foretell or forecast something bad
recluse	*n:* a person who lives in seclusion
reticent	*a:* reluctant to speak; quiet and held back
sanguine	*a:* optimistic, hopeful
supplant	*v:* to take charge by removing someone or something else
temperate	*a:* moderate, reserved (see intemperate)
trepidation	*n:* fear, dread, apprehension
trite	*a:* overused, stale (see banal)
turbulent	*a:* disturbed, disordered, violent
unconventional	*a:* eccentric; not bound by typical rules (see *orthodox*)
vacuous	*a:* not intelligent
venerate	*v:* to respect or look up to
volatile	*a:* unstable; tending toward violence

Print and Online College Admissions Resources

Books

The number of books on college admissions is staggering (and growing daily!). While many offer sound advice, they vary in quality. And some—especially those that promise to get you into a highly selective school—aren't worth your time. The books listed below are the most up-to-date, reliable sources of information.

General Guides

Fiske Guide to Colleges 2011 (Sourcebooks, 2010): Highly recommended; goes beyond statistics to describe the school environment with astounding accuracy. (One important rule for any book you're considering is to check the publication date. Most guides are updated annually, and for good reason. Buy only the most recent version.)

Four-Year College 2011 (Peterson's, 2010): Comprehensive information on every accredited four-year institution in the U.S. and Canada (offering some amazing bargains).

Targeted Info Guide

Colleges that Change Lives: 40 Schools That Will Change the Way you Think About Colleges (Penguin, 2000): Loren Pope's book was groundbreaking when it came out over a decade ago, and now (revised and updated) it's a classic. If you can't get beyond "brand name paralysis," here's where to start.

General Admissions Process

A Is for Admission (Grand Central Publishing, 1999): Advice from the ultimate insider on what really goes on in the admissions offices of highly selective schools. Michele Hernandez reveals the mathematical formula used to rank applicants and offers advice for raising your ranking.

Runner up: For an overview of the current admissions process, get a copy of *The New Rules of College Admissions: Ten Former Admissions Officers Reveal What It Takes to Get Into College Today* (Fireside Books, 2006). Its sound advice and range of topics (extracurriculars, choosing a college, interviews, recommendations) will give you a broad understanding; it's a great place to start.

Finances

Paying for College Without Going Broke 2010 (Princeton Review, 2009). Getting a good deal on a college education is about much more than financial aid, although this book covers that topic well too. Understand how to get tax breaks, negotiate with schools (yes, it can work!), and plan ahead to save before you begin the application process.

Test Practice

The folks who make the ACT and SAT offer actual retired tests so you can gauge your progress. *The Official SAT Study Guide* (College Board, 2004) and *The Real ACT Prep Guide* (Thomson-Peterson's, 2005) are great ways to practice. But these companies don't give too much away. For explanations of question types and strategies, you'll need to look elsewhere.

In-Depth Test Strategy

Don't overlook the importance of understanding how the tests are designed to make you stumble, and find out how to outsmart them. *Up Your Score: The Underground Guide to the SAT* (Workman Publishing, 2008) and *ACT Preparation in a Flash* (LearningExpress, 2006) are the books to turn to for strategy.

Online Resources

Testing

To learn about standardized tests, including what's on them, when they're offered, and how to register, look no further than the sources themselves (other sites contain some information that is not accurate): www.collegeboard.com (SAT) and www.act.org (ACT). Both sites have practice questions, practice tests, and advice for achieving a higher score. If you're taking the SAT, be sure to sign up for the best free test-prep tool around: the SAT Question of the Day, which can be delivered to your inbox every morning, and the site will even keep track of your results.

Don't like your test scores? There are hundreds of test-optional schools that won't ask for your scores. For a list, check www.fairtest.org.

General Admissions Process

Find out what's on college admissions counselors' minds at www.nacacnet.org. The National Association of College Admissions Counseling is made up of those who make the yea or nay decisions, and they share their preferences and experiences in an annual survey. The Student Resources page has a link to buy their Guide for Parents—also worth a look.

Finding a School

There are dozens of college guides online, and the accuracy of information varies widely. If you're into rankings, read first about how they're compiled before you weigh them too heavily. If you have some parameters in mind, such as location, size, major, etc., search sites such as www.petersons.com, www.princetonreview.com, and even www.collegeboard.com. Other sites offer feedback from current students and have message boards where you can share and ask for information and advice. These include www.collegeconfidential.com and collegeprowler.com.

When looking at individual schools' sites, keep in mind that they are designed as marketing tools. The students all look smart, engaged, and fun; and every blade of grass appears to have been manicured by hand. You will get comprehensive information about majors, professors, application dates, and activities, but don't make a decision based on the visuals—or the glowing comments or descriptions.

Paying for School

Get sound financial advice, and apply for federal aid at www.finaid.org. Learn about loans, scholarships, and savings options. Calculators such as a college cost projector and savings plan designer can help you determine what you can afford.

ADDITIONAL ONLINE PRACTICE ▶

Whether you need help building basic skills or preparing for an exam, visit the LearningExpress Practice Center! On this site, you can access additional practice materials. Using the code below, you'll be able to log in and complete two instantly scored SAT essays online. This online essay practice provides you with:

- **Immediate scoring**
- **A detailed scoring guide**
- **Personalized recommendations for further practice and study**

Log on to the LearningExpress Practice Center by using the URL: **www.learnatest.com/practice**

This is your Access Code: **7342**

Follow the steps online to redeem your access code. After you've used your access code to register with the site, you will be prompted to create a username and password. For easy reference, record them here:

Username: _____ **Password:** _____

With your username and password, you can log in and answer these practice questions as many times as you like. If you have any questions or problems, please contact LearningExpress customer service at 1-800-295-9556 ext. 2, or e-mail us at **customerservice@learningexpressllc.com**

NOTES

NOTES

NOTES

NOTES

NOTES

NOTES

NOTES

NOTES